LEADER BOARD

THE DNA OF HIGH PERFORMANCE TEAMS

OMAR L. HARRIS

Leader Board:
The DNA of High-Performance Teams

No team starts out great. There are stages that must be navigated before high performance is truly possible. Unfortunately, many teams never achieve their true potential because leaders don't know how to proactively move groups through these phases. But there are some leaders who have learned to magnify their collective team talent, align and inspire their people, and set ambitious yet achievable targets.

Leader Board: The DNA of High-Performance Teams demonstrates how to discover and unleash the potential of your team's DNA faster and more effectively than ever before. Omar L. Harris creates an impactful new blueprint for team success by synthesizing the stages of group development (forming, storming, norming, performing), and leadership advice from some of the biggest names in business and management into a suite of easily applied team performance acceleration principles.

Level up your team leadership skills by following the fictional story of a pharmaceutical industry leader, Samuel "Coach" Lombardi, who leverages a lifetime of hard-won wisdom to deliver a stellar product launch. After the story, stay for the discussion, where you will gain a treasure chest of ready-made resources to immediately impact your team's performance.

The two most important days in your career are the day you get promoted into leadership and the day you find out *why*. Come inside to unlock the code to making high-performance teams work.

Leader Board: The DNA of High-Performance Teams

by Omar L. Harris

PUBLISHED BY: THE PANTHEON COLLECTIVE (TPC BOOKS)

ISBN: 978-0-9965318-4-9 (ebook)
ISBN: 978-0-9965318-5-6 (paperback)

Author's note

Unless otherwise attributed, all content is the creation of the author or creative collaborator (such as illustrations).

Permissions

Quote on pages 12-13. *Development Sequence in Small Groups* by Bruce Tuckman. ©Copyrights Clearance Center. Used by permission. All rights reserved.

Image on page 133. ***The Five Dysfunctions of a Team: A Leadership Fable*** by Patrick Lencioni. ©John Wiley and Sons 2002. Used by permission. All rights reserved.

Quote on pages 225-26. ***Trust and Betrayal in the Workplace*** by Dennis and Michelle Reina. ©Berrett-Koehler Publishers Inc., 2015. Used by permission. All rights reserved.

Quote on page 256. ***The Four Disciplines of Execution*** by Chris McChesney, Jim Huling, Sean Covey. ©Simon & Schuster. Used by permission. All rights reserved.

TPC Books
pantheoncollective@gmail.com

For Sean M., Ray R., Tracey G., Mike M., Mike Mc., Michael M., Audra R., Kevin C., Stephen M., Rudy S., Peter M., Mark L., Daniel M., Monica J., Sharon B., Charisse E., Kevin S., Ania P-L, Eric C., Panos L., Denise F., Jorge O., Alicia B., Nick B., Veronika L., Glenn A., Brian C., Paramesh N., Duggan C., JD C., Joann A., Scott S., Aresh T., Charles B., Chip D., Dave C., Jon M., Nikki B., Ryan W., Sue I., Rich R., Kate M., Herb E., Tim J., Minesh S., David B., Brian L., Gerry G., Sal G., Karen L., Renee B., Lisa Z., Bill H., Paul M., Jo Ann M., Alexine T., Erica F., Ted G., Lee D., Enrico V., Wendy G., and especially Gaile Keegan
The team that taught me the meaning of team...

And to Tom M., for introducing me to Clifton Strengths®

Contents

FOREWORD: TEAM DNA   11

STORY

  CHAPTER ONE: THE NEGATIVITY TRAP   19

  CHAPTER TWO: TAKE CONTROL   33

  CHAPTER THREE: W.H.O.M.   45

  CHAPTER FOUR: SERVANT LEADERSHIP   55

  CHAPTER FIVE: INTENSE INTENT   65

  CHAPTER SIX: STAR SEARCH   77

  CHAPTER SEVEN: BASIC BRILLIANCE   99

  CHAPTER EIGHT: INFECTIOUS INFLUENCE   117

  CHAPTER NINE: PRODUCTIVE CONFLICT   129

  CHAPTER TEN: KNOW AND OWN YOUR ROLE   137

  EPILOGUE: FOUR WEEKS LATER   151

DISCUSSION

  FORMING   155

  STORMING   191

  NORMING   221

  PERFORMING   261

RESOURCES   265

ACKNOWLEDGMENTS   267

ABOUT THE AUTHOR   273

APPENDIX

  REFERENCES   277

  CHARACTERS   285

FOREWORD: TEAM DNA

I first encountered the concept of team formation in 2005 during a team-building workshop. I was struck by how much sense it made. Teams formed, stormed, normed, and performed. A nice, linear model. Functional.

It was in sophomore biology that I first learned about proteins, RNA, DNA, and genes. I was amazed at how such complexity could emerge from a single cell and how information, form, and function passed vertically from generation to generation. Simplistically, a gene encodes a message to build a protein, therefore enabling information to perform a function. Linear and also functional.

Teams, like genes, exist to perform a function, the success of which results in the achievement (or not) of a given goal. There are a whole host of chemical and biological processes to ensure the proper functioning of genes, but what of the role of the team leaders—the true catalysts of proper team function in the business world? The idea of how to best influence and accelerate team formation and performance has fascinated me ever since I joined my first corporation back in 1998 and continued as I matriculated from individual contributor to team member to enterprise leader. After years of researching and experimentation in the real world, I believe every leader can learn how to effectively accelerate the team-building process and dramatically increase its speed to achieve faster results.

The team-building process was coined by psychologist Bruce Tuckman in his 1965 article, "Developmental Sequence in Small Groups." Tuckman defined the first stage as related to "orientation to the task [known as *forming*], in which group members attempt to identify the task in terms of its relevant parameters and the way the group experience will be used to accomplish the task. The group must decide upon the type of information they will need in dealing with the task and how this information is to be obtained." He continued:

> The second phase in the development of group structure is labeled as intragroup conflict [*storming*]. Group members become hostile toward one another and toward a leader as a means of expressing their individuality and resisting the formation of group structure. Interaction is uneven and "infighting" is common. The lack of unity is an outstanding feature of this phase. There are characteristic key issues that polarize the group and boil down to the conflict over progression into the "unknown" of interpersonal relations or regression to the security of earlier dependence[…]

> The third group structure phase is labeled as the development of group cohesion [*norming*]. Group members accept the group and accept the idiosyncrasies of fellow members. The group becomes an entity by virtue of its acceptance by the members, their desire to maintain and perpetuate it, and the establishment of new group-generated norms to insure

the group's existence. Harmony is of maximum importance, and task conflicts are avoided to insure harmony[...]

The fourth and final developmental phase of group structure is labeled as functional role-relatedness [*performing*]. The group, which was established as an entity during the preceding phase, can now become a problem-solving instrument. It does this by directing itself to members as objects, since the subjective relationship between members has already been established. Members can now adopt and play roles that will enhance the task activities of the group, since they have learned to relate to one another as social entities in the preceding stage. Role structure is not an issue but an instrument which can now be directed at the task. The group becomes a "sounding board" off which the task is "played."

Over the years, I have found that there is a strong correlation between a leader's dedication, focus, and skill in moving his or her team through these four stages and the speed with which the team achieves desired results. I have also found that it can be difficult to connect the dots between advice from leadership gurus and the application of their guidance in the real world. Therefore, I dedicated myself to the task of developing and testing a simple process you can now apply to successfully navigating your teams from forming to performing.

Leader Board: The DNA of High-Performance Teams is a resource that any leader can use to fast-track team development. Consider *Leader Board* a two-for-one—inspiration from the best business minds of the last twenty years combined with an innovative system that puts their ideas and practical experiences to work in the form of Team Performance Acceleration Principles (TPAPs). In the pages that follow, you will be immersed and "edutained" by the fictional story of a leader trying to do something very special with a group of people he is leading. By investing in this story, you will take away actionable wisdom that has been successfully applied in the real world with teams of all sizes, in many different countries and cultural contexts.

Specifically, from this book you will take away *four completely new tools* that I use to navigate every team I lead toward high performance.

- **W.H.O.M.** is an acronym that stands for work-ethic, heart, optimism, and maturity—the basic building blocks I require in every team member I hire. Hopefully, you will find the thirty-two **W.H.O.M.** interview questions as useful as I have as starting points in ensuring you source the right attributes in your key hires.
- As your team is being constructed, **INNERviewing** is an important step in defining your team's *why* based on the individual journeys, needs, motivations, and de-motivators of each person. By aligning each person's *why* with the team's objective, you will gain trust and inspire the collective to be more than the sum of the parts.
- Once the *why* is clear, building the team's **Leader Board**

defines how you can more effectively work together. A **Leader Board** demonstrates who your team leaders should be in terms of getting things done, advocating and elevating standards, ensuring effective ways of working, and solving problems. It will help break down silos and drive greater accountability and productivity. You will find it easy to assemble and activate your own team's DNA via this approach.

- And finally, the fifteen **Team Performance Acceleration Principles (TPAPs)** presented in the discussion section of this book will permit you to meet your team where they are on the journey from forming to performing. Then, you'll learn to masterfully steer your group through the stages faster than ever before.

Every leader can learn how to tap into and unlock their team's DNA to achieve breakout results. Now there is a simple and actionable approach to accelerating teams through the four stages of development: forming, storming, norming, and performing. This approach comes alive through the narrative presented in *Leader Board*. Please enjoy the story and stay for the discussion section, where we will delve specifically into the team-performance acceleration principles (TPAPs), with actionable takeaways and resources you can immediately begin applying with your own teams.

STORY

CHAPTER ONE:
THE NEGATIVITY TRAP

Sam Lombardi's habitual lateness would have been a huge problem if he weren't so good at his job. The problem was that the new senior management of Giant Pharmaceuticals didn't know about his bad habit. It was 7:45 a.m. Sam was running late, as usual, and he'd just learned from his administrative assistant that his new boss, Senior Vice President of Global Marketing Jim Kelly, and the new president of Giant, Carl Reed, wanted to meet with him at nine o'clock.

This was not good. An impromptu meeting first thing Monday morning? It could only mean one thing: Sam's illustrious career at Giant was coming to an end. Sam drove faster. Thankfully, New Jersey's Interstate 295 South was cooperating this morning.

He pulled into the parking garage at 8:43 a.m. and willed his bum knee to move as quickly as he could stand it. When he reached his office on the first floor of the Alexander Building, he found his longtime assistant, Gaile Deegan, waiting. Gaile—reddish blond, five foot three, and full-figured—was a true tough New Jersey gal with Irish roots who'd raised three boys on her own. In her mid-fifties, with twenty-five years of dedicated service to the company under her belt, Gaile was almost as much of a Giant institution as Sam.

"You're sweating, Sam," she said, by way of greeting.

"Good morning to you, too, Gaile," he replied. He noticed that she'd taken a few inches off of her characteristic bob. "Nice hairdo. Is that a new blouse, too?"

"Save the charm for the boys upstairs, Sam," she replied with a smirk. "You're going to need it."

"That bad, huh?"

"Well, the last two people to be summoned for an impromptu meeting with the new boss ended up being escorted off the premises by security. So yeah, I'd be worried."

"Gee, thanks for the pep talk, Gaile."

"You're the coach, Sam. For what it's worth, I hope they don't fire you."

"Me, too," Sam replied. "Now give me a sec to collect my thoughts."

"And straighten your tie."

"Yes, ma'am."

Sam retied his tie and studied his reflection in the mirror on the wall of his office. *When did I get so old?* Thankfully, he still had more black in his full head of hair than gray, but a trace of wrinkles cracked the smooth surface around his eyes. He kept his five-foot-nine frame relatively fit by playing tennis, squash, and golfing whenever his knee would allow, which wasn't often these days—hence the troubling paunch in his abdomen. He remembered his early days as a bright-eyed, bushy-tailed communications manager, before he'd been moved from PR to marketing, where he'd been thriving for the past fifteen years. Would all that come to an end this gloomy Monday morning?

Only one way to find out. Chin high, Sam limped to the elevator and began the longest journey of his twenty-year career.

* * *

Founded in 1847 by American chemists Thomas Finn and Nicolas Edmonton, Giant Pharmaceuticals was one of the oldest pharmaceutical companies in the United States. The fledgling enterprise, originally called Edmonton-Finn, was a holistic medicine company based on the principle that the human body, if given a bit of help, could heal itself. In those days, all business was done at a farmhouse sitting on ten acres of land near the palisades that Thomas Finn had inherited when his father passed away. Today, the corporate headquarters of Giant occupied 240 acres in Washington Township, New Jersey.

After the flu pandemic of 1918, a Greek-American industrialist named Laurence Gigas became intrigued by Edmonton-Finn's alternative medicine approach. He purchased Edmonton-Finn and rebranded the company as *Giant*, after the English translation of his last name. Gigas was inspired by the emergence of vaccination as a paradigm shift in medicine and made it his goal to create the world's largest vaccine producer—a status Giant had definitively obtained by 2016.

Operating in over one hundred fifty markets worldwide,

Giant was also a leader in allergy drugs, antibiotics, antivirals, and, most recently, cardiovascular health with the development of Induet—the world's first safe cholesterol ester transfer protein (CETP) inhibitor—a compound that increased HDL ("good" cholesterol) levels by 40 percent on its own, and in combination with statins (which reduced "bad" cholesterol), lowered total cholesterol scores a whopping 60 percent at the starting dose, thus helping to reduce the risk of heart attack and stroke for high-risk patients. Induet was Sam's baby and had blockbuster drug potential, but previous management had not invested properly in launching the drug and now, twelve months later, the product was plateauing. New management would not want to hear some sob story about the previous team's mismanagement of a product of this magnitude, which pretty much left Sam holding the bag.

With these thoughts on his mind, he entered the expansive lobby of the Magellan Building, which housed human resources (HR), global marketing, finance, and the senior leadership team (SLT). He wiped his forehead with a handkerchief—the hot June air and his own anticipation left him coated with a thin film of sweat. He could only pray his blue shirt was free from unsightly pit stains.

Why am I assuming the worst? Just because Al and John were let go doesn't mean I will be. The launch isn't going so bad—given our level of resources one could argue we're actually overachieving!

Sam stepped into the elevator and pressed the fourth-floor button, reflecting on the book ***How Full Is Your Bucket?*** by the grandfather-grandson team of Donald O. Clifton and Tom Rath. Based on the simple analogy of a ladle and a bucket, their theory stated that each person had an invisible emotional repository, which was continuously being drained or filled by things said and done to, for, or by others. In this way, people were at their best when their emotional bucket was full, and at their worst when their emotional bucket was bare.

Getting out of the elevator, Sam knew the negativity he felt was a result of "empty-bucket syndrome." Negativity was an outlook, energy, and willpower killer because it inspired "give-up-itis." He needed to adjust his attitude quickly or risk carrying this energy into the meeting and creating a self-fulfilling prophecy. Another key element of the ladle/bucket analogy was that whenever a person chose to fill another person's bucket, they in turn filled up their own.

Readers of the book were challenged to take a fifteen-question positive-impact assessment, rating their agreement with statements that reflected how they had interacted with others during the day, including whether they had praised and/or helped their others, noticed the particular expertise of their colleagues, or felt that they made others feel accepted and appreciated in the workplace.

Sam needed to practice praise and knew just whose bucket to fill. He pulled out his cell phone and dialed.

"What did you forget, Sam?" his wife, Patricia, answered.

"I forgot to thank you for the spectacular breakfast you prepared this morning."

"Uh, okay. Are you alright? You complained all morning

that I was making you late."

"I know. I shouldn't have done that. I'm the luckiest man in the world to have you by my side. I don't tell you enough how much I love and appreciate all you do for Michael and me." Sam could tell she was taken off guard by his comments, so he closed the conversation. "Going into a meeting now. Love you."

Sam hung up, imagining the flustered expression on the face of his wife of twenty years. He smiled, feeling fuller already. *Maybe it is better to give than to receive.*

"Morning, Sam," greeted the Afrikaans-accented voice of his new boss, Jim Kelly.

Jim's athletic, six-foot-two-inch physique complemented his commanding presence. Forty-nine years young, Jim ran daily and the only carbs he allowed in his body came from Guiness—his beer of choice. He commuted to Washington Township from Manhattan's Upper West Side, where he lived with his eleven-year-old daughter. Jim had more money than anyone Sam had ever known thanks to his previous job as CEO of a Canadian biotech firm called Jade Pharma (named after his daughter), but his life had been far from easy. Jim's wife had passed away ten years back, so to better focus on raising his daughter, he'd sold Jade Pharma for the cool sum of eighty-six million dollars. Though he was technically set for life, he'd come out of semi-retirement to accept the Senior Vice President position at Giant.

"Morning, Jim," Sam replied, shaking Jim's strong, manicured hand. "How was your weekend?"

"Took Jade to a couple of casting calls," Jim replied. "And I reviewed that brand update you got me so late on Friday."

Uh oh. Sam avoided Jim's intimidating stare. "I'd be glad to walk you through it this morning…"

"Save it. We'll talk after the meeting."

Sam looked up, hopeful. There would be an "after the meeting." That was a good sign.

The secretary interrupted his thoughts. "Carl is ready for you."

But am I ready for this? Sam stood and followed Jim into the conference room.

* * *

Thirty minutes later, Sam limped into Jim's office and sat down across from his still-boss. His head was reeling from the abrupt turn of events. To calm his racing mind, he admired Jim's décor.

The man was quite the minimalist. Not a scrap of paper cluttered his desk; no family pictures on the credenza. In fact, there was only one picture in the room—a framed poster of Winston Churchill. Clearly, Jim patterned himself after the relentless British luminary.

"So, Sam, how are we going to get this done?" Jim asked.

Jim was referring to the mission they'd just received from Carl:

"As we all know, Giant is in significant financial trouble since the loss of our patent on Vyrtex. We're bleeding cash and have nothing in our late-stage pipeline, so we are partnering

with Harris Pharmaceuticals to bring our Induet-Lotor com-
bination product to market. Signed the deal Friday, and the
announcement comes out in an hour. This is a make-it-or-
break-it moment for our company, and we want you to run
the US market, Sam. Get us your initial needs assessment and
budget by the end of the week."

Sam blinked back the memory and cleared his throat.
"Well, the first step is to build out the team. I don't need to
tell you how crucial this is. We've been under resourced since
before we launched Induet last year."

"Agreed," Jim replied. "But I also need your team to
handle Harris. They are known for bullying and outmus-
cling their partners. I need you to bully back. And we have
to get Induet's numbers up. The sales force isn't delivering.
Remember, once we launch the combo you will be the head
of two discrete teams with unique missions – the Induet-Lotor product team and the Induet marketing team. Make some
recommendations there as well."

"Will do, Jim," Sam replied, though he felt that mutual
bullying would be unproductive to both sides. He would
need to find a different path forward. "Thanks for the vote
of confidence."

"You're welcome. Don't make me look like a fool. Oh,
I almost forgot. When you start building out your team, you
should take a look at Dave Maxwell. He's the marketing
director on Taradil."

"I appreciate the recommendation, Jim, but I have a pretty
robust assessment process. We shouldn't just cherry-pick

people for roles, right?"

Jim turned to his computer, signaling the end of the conversation. "I don't care how you assess people, but I expect Dave to be in the mix. He's a difference-maker and I trust him."

Having received the message, Sam exited Jim's office, already putting the action steps in order in his head. Step 1: call a staff meeting. Step 2: call HR to identify internal candidates (and meet up with Dave Maxwell). Step 3: get the needs assessment started.

"How did it go, Coach?" Gaile asked once he was seated at his desk again.

His office was the opposite of Jim's—stacks of paper everywhere, pictures and memorabilia from key moments throughout his career in every available space. The clutter may have created a bad impression, but it was him, through and through.

Sam hung his head, feigning sadness. "Time to get the boxes, Gaile."

Gaile's face fell, but ever the professional, she caught herself and replied, "Will do."

She turned to leave, and Sam stopped her. "Hold on a sec, Gaile. We're gonna need a lot of boxes, because we're moving on up!"

She registered his words and her face widened in a smile.

"We're not going anywhere, Gaile. Call the team in so I can give them the good news!"

* * *

Sam sat at his four-person conference table flanked by his team: Robert Rath and Tanisha Bilal, marketing directors; Alicia Barden, product manager; and Gaile.

"We're done, aren't we?" Tanisha blurted out once everyone was settled in. Coffee-toned with wide, expressive brown eyes, she was the team's resident worrier.

"Is that what everyone thinks?" Sam asked, glancing around the table.

"I'm not assuming anything," Rob said, ever the voice of reason. Rob reminded Sam of a professional newscaster with his broadcasters' baritone and smooth demeanor.

"Come on, Coach," Alicia said. Her trademark enthusiasm was subdued, dulled by the uncertainty. "What's the deal?"

"The deal is," Sam started, "we have a major brand to launch and less than fourteen months to do it."

He watched as a mixture of excitement, fear, and anxiety rippled through everyone's expressions.

"What are we launching?" Rob asked.

"Guess," Sam replied.

"The combo?" Alicia guessed.

She was smart as a whip. A product of the Florida A&M University School of Business and Industry, Alicia had been at Giant a mere three years and had spent just a year on his team but was already indispensable to Sam.

"On the money, as usual, Alicia," Sam replied. "The Indu-et-Lotor combination will soon be a reality."

"There's more, isn't there?" Rob asked. "We're not going it alone, are we?"

Sam glanced at Rob, his right-hand man and the best strategic thinker he'd ever worked with. "Unfortunately not, Rob. A joint venture is being created with Harris Pharmaceuticals."

"Harris?" Tanisha asked incredulously. "There's no such thing as a JV with Harris. They buy every partner they work with."

Tanisha had a point, and she knew firsthand. She'd been working at Medicia when they partnered with Harris to launch a new selective serotonin reuptake inhibitor (SSRI). Within fourteen months, Medicia was acquired by Harris, and 75 percent of the staff, including Tanisha, was laid off.

Sam could see Tanisha's worry and doubt infecting the rest of the group and said, "That's been true in the past, Tanisha, but that outcome is far from a certainty. Either way, that's not our concern now. We need to produce a complete requirements assessment by Friday. Rob, please work with our market research colleagues to draft an initial budget. Tanisha, I need you to evaluate our life cycle management program and recommend enhancements from a data standpoint to bolster our messaging. Alicia, you've got sales force programs— medical education, training needs, etcetera. I'm working on staffing us up to match up with Harris toe-to-toe. Any questions?"

No one spoke, so Sam let them go. Tanisha hung back— clearly, she had something to say that she didn't want everyone to hear. Gaile closed Sam's office door on her way out, giving Tanisha the privacy she desired.

"Everything okay?" Sam asked when they were alone.

"Sam, I don't know how to tell you this," she said.

"By telling me," he replied, warily.

"This was a very difficult decision for me to make but…"

Sam had led enough teams to know what was coming next. Didn't make it any easier though.

"…it's time for me to move on. I'm leaving Giant, Sam."

Sam felt his bucket draining at this news but hoped his face wasn't reflecting it.

"Are you telling me this to allow me to counter offer, or is your mind already made up?" Sam asked.

"If I'm honest, I was on the fence before this meeting, but now I'm definitely decided. I don't want anything to do with Harris! Sorry, Sam."

He stood and gave Tanisha a hug. "Good luck, Tanisha. You will be sorely missed. If you need anything, let me know. And make sure you stay in touch."

As she walked out of his office, Sam sank down hard into his chair. This deal was crucial to the financial future of the company and therefore hinged on delivering the best product launch possible. Meanwhile, most successful product launches usually required thirty-six months of lead time to fully deliver the requisite combination of insight, strategy, resourcing, execution, and belief. The fourteen months he'd been given were already pushing the limits of reality, and now he had to deal with breaking in new people? His mental pressure dial turned from intense to extreme.

Sam dug through the mountain of paper on his desk and

found the "positive impact test" questions from ***How Full Is Your Bucket?*** He needed to do some more bucket filling to balance his emotional state. His eyes fixated on statement number six: *"I am more productive when I am around positive people."* That brought his mind back to Dave Maxwell. With Tanisha's exit, there was now a marketing director spot open.

Sam had interacted with Dave on a few occasions and although he didn't know much about his marketing acumen, Dave had a reputation for generosity and positivity. He pinged Gaile. "Please get Dave Maxwell on the line."

CHAPTER TWO:

TAKE CONTROL

Forming - Fourteen months to launch

Sam set his briefcase down in the hallway of his four-bed-room, four-bathroom, Tudor-style domicile in Princeton, New Jersey. The house was filled with the delicious smell of his wife's famous Bolognese sauce. Sam's stomach growled.

"What a day," Sam said, giving Patricia a peck on the lips.

"You look shell-shocked, honey," Patricia said.

"Fitting, since that's exactly how I feel."

"Well, fix your face. Michael is having some problems of his own and needs his father's ear."

Sam nodded and adjusted his attitude accordingly. Heading up to his son's room, he wondered what could be going on with Michael. When he was fourteen, the biggest worries Sam could recall revolved around the confusion and inconveniences of puberty and, of course, girls. What he'd give to swap the problems of adolescence for the pressures and challenges of adult life that seemed to continually expand with age. Concern and anxiety had become his daily foes.

He rapped on Michael's door. "Hey Michael, open up."

A moment later, Sam stood face-to-face with his teenage son, who appeared to be trying to block whatever he'd been doing in his bedroom. Sam's eyes darted inside and saw the iPad and earbuds on Michael's rumpled bedspread. Michael's current "thing" was hip-hop culture, and the walls were covered with posters and artwork of his favorite indie rap artists (many with names Sam could barely pronounce). Bordering a bit on OCD, Michael made certain that everything in his room had a preferred place and was well organized—from his dirty clothes (one hamper for regular clothes, another for under-garments) to his book collection (filed on his bookshelf not by author, but by subject matter).

"What's up, Dad?"

"Plenty, Son, but I want to know what's up with you. How's high school treating you these days?"

"Okay. Nothing I can't handle."

"I'm sure. Anything happen lately that I should know about?"

"Not really… Oh, I made the freshman basketball team."

"That's fantastic, Michael! Congrats! Were you worried you wouldn't make it?"

"Nope. But that's the problem. State rules say they're not allowed to cut any kids who try out for the team."

"So, every kid who went out made the team?" Sam asked.

"Yup. All thirty of us."

"Wow," Sam replied. "That's a huge team!"

Michael looked away. "Probably won't be for long. At practice today, the coach went on this rant about how stupid the rule is and how it was his mission to make eighteen of us quit. He said the Survivor Series begins tomorrow…"

"And you're worried you'll be one of the eighteen, right?"

Michael nodded.

"Hmmm… Your coach sounds like a pretty short-sighted fellow. Instead of taking the time to find out what every player can do on the court, he'd rather spend his energy trying to run you kids off the team. What are you going to do?"

"Don't know. Part of me wants to drop out now. But another part wants to prove Coach wrong…"

In Michael's tone, Sam heard a need for some direction, so he said, "I've been where you are, Son. My advice is to take the action that gives you the most control."

Sam had once attended a seminar given by Stephen R. Covey, author of *The 7 Habits of Highly Effective People*. The part of Covey's talk that resonated most was his discussion of the first habit—*Be Proactive*. Proactivity, in Covey's definition, was about taking responsibility and control over one's own life, and more specifically controlling one's response to stimuli. "Behavior, basically, is a function of decisions and not conditions," Covey had said.

According to Covey, there were two types of people in the world: proactive and reactive. Reactive people allowed external conditions to control their behaviors, whereas proactive people controlled their behaviors and actions by minimizing the effects of negative conditions. The key was to be self-aware enough to decide whether "to act or be acted upon." This concept was illustrated using the metaphor of three circles: concern, influence, and control.

In Covey's methodology, people generally experienced problems caused by three types of issues: direct control, indirect control, and no control. The first, direct control, related to personal issues regarding one's own behavior, or things within one's own direct control. These types of problems existed in a "Circle of Control." The second circle is the "Circle of Influence," where issues over which one has indirect control—like problems with the behavior of others—exist. The final and largest circle, the "Circle of Concern," is where problems of over which one has no control are located. These involve things that cannot be changed, such as the past or the future.

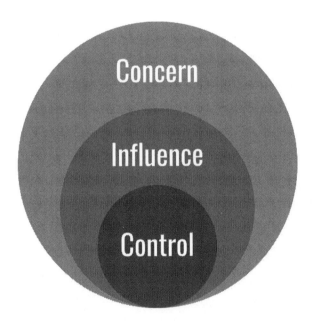

Seeing an opportunity to make an impression on Michael using Covey's tactics, Sam went into "Coach" mode.

"Let me ask you something," he started. "These days, do you feel like you have more worries and problems than you have things under your control?"

Always a thoughtful boy, Michael considered the question for a moment before responding. "Of course. I've got tons of worries and problems…"

By the way he trailed off, Sam knew not to probe. Instead he said, "Me, too, Son. Me, too. And such is the nature of life that our worries and problems always outnumber the things we feel are within our control. However, if we can manage to focus on what we *do* control, we can minimize the power of the things we don't. Does that make sense to you?"

Michael slowly nodded.

"So, what do you feel you *can* control these days?"

"Basically nothing, Dad. My coordination is off. I can't get the girl I like to notice my existence, and I can't even play the game I love because of my dumb coach." He was clearly downcast.

Sam needed to pick Michael back up and fill his bucket. "I know it may feel that way, Michael, but you have more control than you may think." He paused for effect. "Have you ever heard the expression 'attitude is everything'?"

Michael nodded.

"Well, it's completely true." Sam recounted the story of how his day had gone. "As soon as I shifted my attitude toward the meeting, everything changed for me. Easier said than done, I know, but if you can master this at your age, you will be brilliantly happy and massively productive at the same time. Your coach may be in charge, but he doesn't know what you know."

"What do I know?" Michael asked, clearly exasperated.

"You know how hard you are willing to work to become the best basketball player you can be. You also know that no matter what the coach does to you, he can't make you quit. He doesn't know how mentally tough you are."

Michael dropped his eyes for a long while, and Sam thought he'd lost him.

Finally, Michael raised his head and a cautious smile appeared. "Okay. I get your point. This is a battle of wills, right? As long as I keep mine strong, I can't lose."

Sam beamed. "Exactly! So, what are you going to do?"

"Focus on what I can control. Practice hard and stay upbeat about the process," Michael replied.

After his own eventful day, Sam nearly got teary eyed but instead held out his fist. "That's right."

Michael fist-bumped him.

"Do you know the three most powerful words in the English language, Son?"

Michael shrugged. "Dunno."

"*Can, will,* and *do* on the positive side. And *can't, won't,* and *don't* on the negative side."

"That's six words."

"Whatever. You get my point?"

"I guess so. If I *can* do something, then I should by exerting my *will* and *doing* my best?"

"Who's the man?" Sam said, giving him a hug.

* * *

The next day, Sam's concerns were piling up. With four days until he had to make his team structure proposal to senior management, everything was going against him. Tanisha had called out (presumably to meet her new employer), there was a system glitch in HR preventing him from accessing the internal talent pool database, Jim was pressing him for a preview of the plan, and it was raining—which always made his knee pain worse. On the bright side, Gaile had called in a favor with an admin friend at Harris and had obtained a copy of Harris's cardiovascular team's structure. Staring at the organizational chart made him anxious; Harris had three times the number of people of his current team.

How am I supposed to justify a team of this size? he asked himself.

He was ready to throw in the towel when Alicia showed up at his door.

"Hey, Coach, got a minute?"

"For you, Alicia, I've got five."

"Excellent. I've been doing some research with our sales colleagues on Harris's performance in the field…"

"Go on," Sam replied, leaning forward.

"Although they basically invented the lipid-lowering category, they are getting their butts kicked in terms of execution metrics. They reach and sample less doctors than their competitors, conduct less speaker programs, and have a lower sales per representative than key benchmarks.

"How do we know this?" Sam challenged.

"I was able to get my hands on secondary data and then I cross-referenced it with what I was hearing from our reps."

A lightbulb went on in Sam's head. This was it! "Alicia, you are a genius!"

"I am?" Alicia asked.

"Definitely! I've been sitting here trying to find an angle to justify more resources, and you just handed it to me on a platter!"

"I'm happy you're happy, Coach. But I'm not sure I follow."

"It's okay, Alicia. I'm not being completely clear. Can you get me that data ASAP? All will be explained soon."

"Will do, Coach." She left the room.

Sam wanted to dance. Harris was weak where Giant was strong, and vice versa. They didn't need an internal arms race. They needed to complement each other and each do what their side did best. Sam began to draft an organizational structure. As he progressed, his concerns melted away.

* * *

The next day he presented the structure proposal to Jim.

"At first, I was worried about all the things Giant didn't know about competing in this space," Sam admitted, presenting a list of concerns. "But then I realized that our knowledge deficit didn't matter because Harris knows *everything* about this category."

Jim lifted an eyebrow at this.

"I know what you may be thinking, Jim, but please indulge me for a moment. Harris launched the first two cholesterol lowering agents, prepped the market, educated clinicians, conducted the landmark clinical trials, and built strong relationships with key opinion leaders worldwide. They also have very high patient usage, leading to significant brand awareness. Due to all this effort, they have built quite a large circle of influence in the world of cholesterol management."

Sam revealed a slide that contained a graphic titled "Harris Circle of Influence" and then clicked to reveal a significantly smaller "Giant Circle of Influence."

Harris Circle of Influence
- Key opinion leaders
- Scientific evidence
- Leading products in the category
- Significant clinician experience
- Continual investment
- Clinician education efforts
- High public brand awareness

Giant Circle of Influence
- Clinical investigators involved in Induet trials
- Moderate clinician experience

"It would be foolhardy to say that we can be more influential on the market than Harris in the short term, wouldn't you agree?"

Jim gave a slight nod in assent.

Sam clicked to a new slide, which depicted a declining

market share trend over the past three years.

"Harris's biggest concerns, however, are that since the launches of key competitors Primator and Zetator, Lotor's market share has steadily declined year after year," he stated. "Now, it's only the third-leading agent in a class of four. They haven't been acting on the correct areas to drive their business in the right direction, and that's where we come in. Look at this comparison."

Sam advanced to Alicia's slide, showing a side-by-side comparison between Harris's executional sales force metrics across multiple brands versus Giant's executional sales force metrics for their key brands. Giant clearly beat Harris at every single important performance indicator for sales force effectiveness.

"Harris may have significant influence in this category," Sam explained, "but they haven't demonstrated the will to win in this very competitive environment by improving their sales force effectiveness."

He progressed to a new slide.

Harris Circle of Control

- Representative product and disease training
- Competitive share of voice
- Process driven

Giant Circle of Control

- Representative product and disease training
- Manager product and disease training
- Selling-skills clinics
- Competitive share of voice
- Performance-driven
- Aligned and tracked sales-effectiveness metrics
- Strong managed care relationships
- Root cause analysis, problem identification and escalation

"Jim, I know you asked me to create a structure that matches them toe-to-toe, but is that the most productive way to operate? If we can marry our performance-driven approach with Harris's ability to influence the environment, I think we can create a win-win scenario that demands half the resources they have, with three times the impact."

"If you can get the right people," Jim stated.

"Exactly," Sam replied. "And not only that, but they have to have the right set of capabilities to really make an impact on this partnership."

Jim sat back in his chair for a while and mulled over the proposal. Sam forced himself to keep his mouth shut and let the man think.

Finally, Jim said, "I'm supportive, Sam, and I think senior leadership will be too—once we tighten up the story a little bit. I want you to punch up the bit around Harris's lack of executional excellence so they can't help but get the point. And now that I see what you need, I expect you to move on Dave Maxwell's offer, ASAP. He's the executional leader you will need to pull this off."

"I spoke with Dave yesterday, and I agree, Jim. He's going to make a great addition to the team. I'll revise the presentation and get it to you before the end of the day. Thanks again for all your support!"

"Don't thank me yet, Sam. This thing could go either way. Still, it's a good start."

CHAPTER THREE:

W.H.O.M.

Forming - Thirteen months to launch

One month had passed since senior management approved his structure proposal, and Sam had spent countless hours evaluating internal candidates with little return on his efforts. Jim was getting impatient and questioning Sam's every decision, but Sam stuck to his guns. He refused to be rushed in his quest to build out a winning team.

There was nothing worse than making the wrong hire. A few years back, against the advice of HR director and good friend Chuck Towns, Sam hired a product manager from a well-established pharma company instead of bringing in a marketer with a consumer goods background. Skills-wise and fit-wise, the consumer goods marketer was the superior candidate, but Sam didn't feel he had the time to train up someone from outside pharma, so he downplayed the pharma marketer's gaps—mainly that he had poor communication skills and a reputation for being territorial on teams.

A year later, when the manager Sam hired missed his tenth crucial deadline due to focusing on something he thought was more important, Sam realized that Chuck had been right in his assessment. The rest of Sam's team was revolting because of how poorly this person communicated. After discovering that this employee was misusing company funds on business trips, Sam fired him. Unfortunately, the superior candidate was thriving in a new job by that time and had no interest in joining Giant. Sam learned the hard way how costly a bad hire could be, and he vowed never to make that mistake again. The costs to productivity, finances, morale, and reputation were far too expensive to bear.

Good to Great by Jim Collins—generally seen as one of the most influential business books of the early twenty-first century—provided Sam with the key principle he needed to avoid pitfalls in hiring. Collins argued that great leaders and great companies should focus on getting the right people on board, *then* on determining in which direction to move—a principle he called "First Who, Then What." This principle could help ensure that an existing team was comprised of the critical capabilities needed to win, as well as guide a leader in hiring the right people in the first place.

Good to Great was one of Sam's all-time favorite business books. It had helped him understand the importance of finding the right people for a team before choosing that team's strategic direction. Step One: slow down the recruitment process. Giant typically hired or promoted people from within based on recommendations and screening interviews, but there was only so much that could be gleaned from a review of a candidate's resume and reference checks. Resumes were marketing documents designed to camouflage flaws and oversell candidates' experience, and references were usually nothing more than loyal friends who would say anything to help their buddies.

Sam had developed identified a method for choosing his kind of people and assimilated it into an acronym—**W.H.O.M.**, which stood for **W**ork Ethic, **H**eart, **O**ptimism, and **M**aturity. The best teams he had been a part of were those on which everyone worked diligently toward objectives, shared a passion for their work, sought solutions rather than succumbing to obstacles, and had the maturity to navigate inevitable disappointments and conflicts without losing focus on shared goals. The **W.H.O.M.** methodology helped him find the true diamonds in the rough. Candidates progressed from a resume screening focused on identification of skills, to a behavioral panel designed to assess that their values fit the team's requirements. Next, they would present a business case so the hiring committee could get a glimpse of their thought process, concluding with a **W.H.O.M.** interview with Sam.

Sam liked to interview candidates over a meal—usually lunch at a restaurant nearby. Sam found that candidates relaxed over food, which allowed him to examine everything from their table manners to how friendly they were with the waitstaff. (Sam once dismissed a highly recommended candidate because he'd yelled at a waitress for mixing up his order.)

Sam had developed a list of questions to assess the elements of **W.H.O.M.** while interviewing.

Work Ethic	Heart	Optimism	Maturity
How do you judge a successful day?	What are your reasons for doing your best every day?	Describe the most stressful work situation you have encountered and how you handled it.	Describe a situation where you had an argument with a co-worker
How do your teammates rate you in terms of getting things done?	What are some of your hobbies and interests outside of work?	Tell me about a time when your superior came to you with a problem they wanted you to fix but you didn't knowhow, or waht to do.	Describe a situation whereyou were right but still had to follow instructions.
Tell me about a time when you overcame a significant challenge to finish a project on schedule.	What's one thing you're really proud of and why?	What are the biggest failures of your career so far?	Talk about a time when one of your ideas was challenged by colleague. What happened?
Describe a situation when you had to work as a member of a team to complete a task.	If we were to hire you, what do you seeing yourself doing here in three years?	Why do you think you willbe successful in this position?	Tell me about the most difficult decision you had to make recently.
Tell me about a time your workday ended before you were able to finish your tasks.	How have you helped others outside of work?	Give me an example where you helped a teammate achieve a goal where there was nothing in it for you.	How do you calm yourself down when you feel anxious or upset?
How do you remind yourself to complete projects and tasks?	Give me an example of something that you have focus on that took great courage and hard work to overcome.	Discuss a problem in your current role which you have yet to solve.	Tell me about a recent time a colleague disappointed you yet you still had to work together to complete a task.
When you have a lot of work to do, how do you get it all done? Give an example.	What excites you most about this opportunity?	Describe a situation where you had to collaborate with a difficult colleague.	Describe to me your biggest weakness and biggest strength.
Describe a situation when personal issues pulled you away from work and how you handled it?	What's the most fun you've ever had at work?	What do you do to de-stress?	Tell me about a colleague you really got along with and why you think you did.

He always asked at least sixteen of the thirty-two questions. Work ethic queries assessed a candidate's reliability, dedication, productivity, cooperation, and self-discipline. Heart probes assessed a candidate's values, motivators, outside interests, career goals, energizers, generosity, and courage.

Optimism inquiries assessed a candidate's solution orientation, agility, flexibility, judgment, curiosity, and resilience. Maturity questions reflected a candidate's capability to make difficult decisions, handle conflict, build productive relationships, and manage negative emotions.

Over time, Sam noticed there was an inverse relationship between where someone went to school (Ivy Leaguers being some of the worst offenders) and their work ethic scores in his interviews. Ivy League graduates did reasonably well in terms of reliability and self-discipline, but generally scored poorly in the areas of dedication, productivity, and cooperation. Many were individual stars who didn't mesh well with the team concept, and only worked hard if they received substantial recognition (and/or compensation) for their efforts.

Sam liked working with smart folks but preferred those who knew how to put their heads down and get the job done for the sake of doing a good job, not just to score points with the boss. He also knew that this belief created a limiting bias against so-called "elite" intellectual talents, so he tried to balance this bias out via the other criteria of heart, optimism, and maturity.

Such was the case with interviewee number twelve: Lincoln Stephens, a thirty-year-old ELITE associate. The ELITE associate program was Giant's fast-track leadership-development program for superstar MBAs. Lincoln was two years out of Duke University's Fuqua School of Business, where he'd received his MBA with a focus on health-sector management. His undergraduate degree was from Oxford

University in England, where he'd grown up. He spoke very deliberately with a soft British accent that forced you to lean in to hear him properly, but he looked like a lanky Brad Pitt.

Lincoln had performed well in the preceding three stages of the process and came with a glowing recommendation from Alicia. Still, without her vote of confidence, Sam would never have given this guy a second glance. His resume screamed "arrogant prick," and his outward appearance and quiet confidence only confirmed that assumption. But Alicia vouched for him, so Sam was compelled to give him an honest chance. Unfortunately, he'd only received an average score on Sam's work ethic assessment, which didn't bode well for the rest of the interview. Sam rated the quality of the responses to each question on a scale of one to five; an average score was twelve or less in any of the four categories of **W.H.O.M.**

"Okay, Lincoln," Sam said as their entrées arrived. "Now I'd like to move on to another set of questions, if you don't mind."

"Of course not, Sam. Please, go right ahead."

Lincoln still spoke in that cool tone, but Sam could tell he'd rattled him a bit with questions about how his teammates would rate him and how he judged a successful day.

"Tell me about some of your passions. What motivates you to do your best every day?"

Lincoln pushed up his glasses and responded, "Well, Sam, that would have to be my children and my beautiful wife."

This was the kind of information you'd never get from a standard CV screening. "How many kids do you have?" Sam asked.

"Six-year-old twins—a boy and girl," Lincoln replied, smiling. "Want to see a picture?" He pulled out his smartphone (with the original *Star Trek* cast on the back of the protective cover), unlocked the screen, and revealed two beautiful, brown-haired kids with slightly Asian features. "My wife is Japanese," he continued anticipating the question he saw forming on Sam's face. "My son, Kent, was just diagnosed with Asperger's Syndrome—you know the autism-spectrum disorder?"

"Yes," Sam replied, thinking of his best friend's youngest daughter. "And I know how tough that can be on a family."

"It's definitely been a challenging situation, but my wife and I consider ourselves very blessed. We underwent fertility treatments for two years before the twins were conceived. Those miracle babies are our world. Protecting and providing for them is my primary motivation in life."

"I can relate," Sam replied, a little thrown off by the turn in the conversation. To regain his balance he said, "Okay, let's switch gears a bit. Describe to me your biggest weakness and biggest strength."

Lincoln put his phone down and thought for a long moment. Sam liked that he considered questions before diving into answers.

Finally, Lincoln said, "In terms of biggest strength, I think I'm pretty good at making strategic choices based on insight into a projected future trend or pattern. I can anticipate three to four steps ahead and usually make the right decisions in the now."

"You must make for a formidable chess opponent," Sam remarked with a chuckle. "Remind me never to play against you."

"I am fairly good at chess," Lincoln said. "In terms of my biggest weakness, I would have to say influencing others has always been a bit of a challenge for me. I'm good at providing options, but when I really need to convince someone to follow my lead, I sometimes fall short."

"Very interesting," Sam replied. "In what ways have you learned how to manage with this weakness and not let it derail your progress?"

"Well, to be honest, Sam, I think I still have a long way to go. That's one of the reasons I'm keen to join this team. I've heard from Alicia that your influencing capabilities are second to none. Learning from others has always been the best way for me to develop in my weaker areas in the past, and I hope to get the chance to learn from you."

"Fair enough," Sam said. Now it was time to throw his subject off. "Give me an example of something that you have focused on that took great courage and hard work to overcome." This was Sam's standard final question, used to assess a candidate's rating against the Heart parameter of the **W.H.O.M.**

Once again, Lincoln mulled it over before responding. "The hardest thing about being the parent of an autistic child has been the realization that the things I do best in the workplace—long-range planning and strategizing—are basically useless in the day-to-day management of the things that make my son's life difficult. I have had to really focus on finding solutions beyond myself, as well as having the courage to depend on the strengths of others while remaining optimistic and flexible. Having a wonderful child like Kent has been the greatest gift of my life. It has enhanced my purpose, made me aware and appreciative of my limitations, and taught me patience and gratitude for each moment…"

Sam was dumbfounded. He had not expected such a vulnerable, yet powerful, response. Sam hadn't yet received the formal assessment from the panel that had reviewed Lincoln, but he trusted his instincts. He needed this young man on his team.

"Wow. Great answer, Lincoln. Thank you for your candor. How soon can you start?"

CHAPTER FOUR:
SERVANT LEADERSHIP

Forming - Twelve months to launch

The combo now had a brand name—Goltur—and Sam's team build-out was progressing well. Dave Maxwell was officially on board and Sam put him in charge of operational excellence. Jim had turned out to be spot-on about Dave, who was proving to be an incredible asset to the team.

"Hey, Sam," Dave greeted, popping his head into Sam's office. "How's it going?"

"I've had better days." Sam had been at his desk for over an hour working on an email for Myra Khan, the CEO of Giant. She had received a letter from an irate patient and enlisted Sam's help to craft a response. Since Myra sat at the very top of the Giant food chain, when she needed something, you dropped everything to attend to it.

"Whatcha working on?" Dave asked, looking over his shoulder. Unbeknownst to Sam, Dave had crossed the room and was now standing behind the desk, gazing at the screen. Dave reminded Sam of a cross between Bill Murray and John Candy. He had Candy's physicality with Murray's deadpan sense of humor and perfect comedic timing.

Not used to this level of professional intimacy, Sam was

about to say something about the importance of personal space when he noticed Dave's body language. Dave was focused, radiating positive energy, and clearly looking to help. *He's a natural bucket filler*, Sam thought. And frankly, he'd hit a wall and could use some help.

"I'm struggling to find the right words to respond to this patient concern about the packaging for Induet," Sam said.

"Can I see the letter?"

Sam turned it over, and Dave read it twice. "Seems like she has a point, right?"

"What do you mean?"

"Well, isn't the customer always right? This elderly woman is having problems opening our blister packs. Instead of confusing her with some corporate BS, shouldn't we just tell her that we'll investigate the packaging situation and try to make it easier to open in the future? We should offer to pay for her meds, too, as thanks for raising this issue. What do you think?"

"I don't know if that will fly with senior management, Dave. But I like the patient-focused approach. Let's try it." Sam finished the email and invited Dave to join him for lunch.

Turns out, Myra *loved* Dave's proposal and sent Sam a personal note of thanks for the excellent customer response. Moving forward, she planned to utilize this approach across all product lines.

Lincoln had joined the team soon after Dave, and very quickly things came together on the structure front. To lead communications, Sam hired Rebecca Abrams, a sales force leader with marketing experience. Marcus Gleeson, another ELITE associate, would join the team in a few weeks as a market access manager. Sam derived immense pleasure from his soon-to-be-completed organizational chart. He had the right mix of youthful exuberance, strategic thinking, and field experience to match up to Harris's marketing prowess.

Meanwhile, the tasks and pressure mounted. With only twelve months before launch, a ton of deliverables rested on their collective plate. Sam was getting ready to sit down and develop a plan of action when he noticed an Amazon package on his desk.

Sam checked the name of the sender. The package was from Tanisha. Losing her had been an unexpected blow, but Dave, despite his lack of category experience, was turning out to be something of an upgrade.

Gaile entered the office with some documents for him to sign. "What did Tanisha send you?"

"I don't know yet."

"Well, are you going to open it or stare at it?"

Sam ripped open the box and found a book inside. The title, ***The Servant: A Simple Story About the True Essence of Leadership***, leapt out at him. Sam wondered what Tanisha was trying to tell him with her parting shot. Then he saw a note:

Coach,

I'm sure you're raising your eyebrows at the title of this book. I read this recently and as I turned the pages, I couldn't help but think of how much you embody these

principles. I hope you will accept this gift in the spirit in which it was intended—simply an acknowledgment of one of my favorite leaders. I won't miss Giant, but I will miss you!
    All the best—please stay in touch.
    Tanisha

Sam was taken aback. Tanisha had always kept her own counsel and had not opened up or engaged with him or the team to the extent he would have liked, but she'd served the business well, and he would miss her too.

Sam examined the book. According to the back cover copy, the book centered on a successful businessman named John Daily, who was failing his family as a husband and father, and also failing as a coach and boss. John decided to attend a week-long leadership retreat at a remote Benedictine monastery, where he met a former Wall Street legend turned monk who showed him a different perspective on leadership: servant leadership.

Intrigued, Sam resolved to add the book to his October reading list. Seven years earlier, after experiencing a near career collapse and nervous breakdown, he'd made the commitment to reading two books per month to facilitate self-improvement. This practice had helped him evolve through a career low and completely turned his professional life around.

Before his tenure at Giant's Washington Township corporate headquarters, he'd been given the opportunity to run Giant's Animal Health business unit in Canada. The position was a huge step up from his previous post, but it meant Sam and Patricia would have to pack up their cozy New Jersey lives and head up to the great white north.

Up to that point, Sam hadn't managed anyone, nor had he owned a P&L (profit and loss) statement—the ultimate scorecard of business financial performance. Sam started his new position with excitement and enthusiasm, but soon found himself out of his depth in both his personal and professional spheres. At work, he was dealing with a product manager loaded with bad habits and lacking key basic capabilities like sales forecasting, which led to a market shortage of his leading product and a declining sales trend. His sales team lacked leadership and executional focus, and his boss was a bit aloof to Sam's challenges, expecting him to magically "fix it" all. At home, Patricia was having trouble adjusting to Quebec, and Michael was struggling in his new school as well. It wasn't long before Sam felt like he was drowning under the weight of combined responsibility.

Sam needed direction, a life preserver, but there had been no ex–Wall Street leadership guru turned monk to guide him back to shore. Sam's resurgence came because of two key realizations: 1) he hated being called "the boss," and 2) he was not doing a very good job managing his time and energy. Being new to management and supervision, he had mistakenly believed that being the boss meant directing everyone's traffic and doing their job for them. This left little time for the things that filled up his bucket—mainly spending quality time with his wife and son, watching sports, playing golf, and reading for learning and pleasure. As he grew more frustrated and depleted, productivity stalled.

He was miserable, stuck in a lose-lose situation. Something had to give.

The solution came after he broke down in front of his wife after a particularly tough day. Patricia listened to him vent about his struggles, then issued a simple challenge—push accountability away from himself and support his people to establish and meet standards.

"Stop being Donkey Kong," she said.

"Donkey Kong?"

"Yes! You are standing on top of your organization tossing flaming barrels down to your team, who can't dodge, jump, or destroy them. You need to be down there on the bottom with your team, helping them to see the barrels, climb the ladders, anticipate the attacks, and use their hammers. Then *Donkey Kong* becomes a game you are collectively playing as you work to ascend together."

Sam stared at his wife in wonder, amazed at her insights. He wasn't the head of his organization; the mission was to beat Donkey Kong. He needed to be down in the trenches, leading his team by directing, coaching, enabling, and empowering them. This shift would allow him to kill the "boss" label and operate in more of an inverted triangle hierarchy, where the value creators in his organization would occupy the boss seats and the rest of the team, himself included, would exist to support their success.

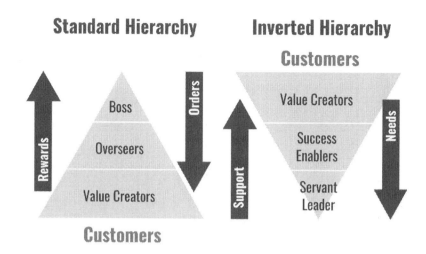

After this talk with Patricia, he'd created buttons for his staff, depicting inverted triangles to remind them who they worked for—who was on top. It took constant reinforcement of the concept for his team to get it, but eventually they followed his lead. In this inverted hierarchy, the manager no longer occupied a privileged position of power over others; the manager was an enabler of success for the company's frontline value creators. Sam's job as a servant leader was to make sure he understood the needs and challenges of his success enablers and value creators and consistently supported them in overcoming their challenges and achieving their goals.

This revelation changed Sam's career. From that moment forward, he dedicated himself to acquiring the leadership tools that would allow him to best serve his teams—specifically by giving great feedback and coaching people. One of his staff members started calling him Coach, and the reputation and nickname stuck.

Sam took a moment to reflect on whether he was directing or enabling his current team. Due to the pressures of the launch, he'd been doing a lot more dumping than uplifting and inspiring great performance. Tanisha's gift was a fantastic reminder that his job was to lead by serving the needs of his people. He thought of some of his most recent frustrations with team members, then flipped the scenarios from what he wanted and expected to what they needed to be successful. Through this lens, he quickly saw the calibrations he needed to make to support and serve them better.

One of his immediate actions would be to sponge ideas from this new book!

Sam put the book in his portfolio bag and glanced up to see Dave and Lincoln at his door. They had a catch-up scheduled for two p.m.

"Come on in, guys," he said, taking a seat at the conference table. "How is the sales force optimization work going?"

"Slow!" Dave replied, taking a seat. "Our sales force structure vendor is sucking gas—way behind where they should be. We just met with them and gave some colorful feedback. They agreed to speed the heck up, but even in the best-case scenario, they will still finish a week behind schedule."

"They weren't fully transparent about their capacity at the beginning of the project," Lincoln interjected.

"That's no good," Sam said. "I'll get on the phone with Bob Jackson, their CEO, and make sure he meets his commitments."

"I'm not sure that's necessary, Sam," Dave said. "We've got it under control."

"No doubt, Dave," Sam replied. "I'm not calling Bob as an indictment of something you're not doing. My job is to support us in achieving key deliverables, and I can best support in this situation by going straight to the top on this issue and providing some air support for my guys. Make sense?"

Dave and Lincoln nodded, noticeably more relaxed.

"Well, while you've got him on the phone, Sam, can you also get us a few courtside tickets to the Knicks-Cavs game?" Dave deadpanned.

"Very funny, Dave. Now get out of my office so I can make this call."

CHAPTER FIVE:

INTENSE INTENT

Forming and Storming – Ten months to launch

It was put-up-or-shut-up time. The team's first business review was imminent.

If product launches were the equivalent of the Super Bowl, then business reviews with senior management were like "win or go home" playoff games. The previous management team at Giant had once fired a senior marketing director over a terrible presentation. This was an extreme example, but it did up the stakes for Sam's new team's first time under the microscope. Senior management would use this two-hour boardroom presentation to assess the team's analytical rigor, strategic thinking, detail orientation, and drive for results. The team would either establish themselves as credible and worthy of continued empowerment, or they would falter and the level of scrutiny from the top would intensify tenfold, making work unbearable.

Sam welcomed the challenge because he loved public speaking and the performance aspect of boardroom presentations. He'd been a theater kid in high school and was comfortable onstage. There was something special about the moment just before engaging with an audience—the way anticipation manifested into an almost tangible presence in the room, the performer's thudding heartbeat intermingling with the excited whispers of a packed crowd. Openings were key, for in every opening there was a promise or intent established with the participants. What was this all going to be about? Would it be a waste of time, or would something valuable be offered?

In his corporate life, Sam had learned a simple rule of effective communication: the clearer the intent for communicating, the more likely key messages could be decoded by one's audience. He built this idea out further upon reading ***Everyone Communicates, Few Connect***, a book by his all-time favorite leadership guru, John C. Maxwell. According to Maxwell, effective leaders understood five key principles of connection and applied five key practices: Connection increased a leader's influence by focusing on the perspectives and needs of others, paying attention to verbal and non-verbal cues, putting the required energy into creating and maintaining the connection, and improving one's skill at connecting through study and practice. In terms of practice, excellent connectors worked to find commonalities, were adept at keeping things simple, cultivated positive experiences, inspired listeners, and walked the talk.

Sam had synthesized this advice into a game-tested formula for preparing business reviews. It all started with a discussion of "the story." Sam approached business reviews like he was crafting a bestselling novel—a catchy opening, a dramatic climax, and a conclusion with key asks for support from senior leaders.

"So, what's the story this time around, Coach?" Alicia had asked at the start of their first preparation meeting. She was responsible for compiling the deck.

"What do you mean, *story*?" Rebecca interjected with her Atlanta twang.

"The story is like the theme of the presentation," Alicia responded.

"The theme," Sam added, "and the through-line that connects the dots from beginning to end. Don't worry, we're not crafting some fanciful tale or fable. It's important that whatever we present is an honest and transparent review of current performance, priorities, good practices, issues, risks, and opportunities. But these must be framed in the most digestible fashion possible, hence the *story*. Make sense?"

Rebecca nodded.

"Good. I've spoken to Jim to gain insight into what Myra and company will be looking to dig into this round. It's straightforward. They are expecting an update on launch prep for Goltur, and more specifically, they want to understand more about the market landscape and get a sense of how we should price this novel therapy."

"For those of you who are new to this process, let me break it down," Alicia said, taking over. "We need to assess where we are against all our key deliverables, identify the current issues, and crystallize what's working, what's not, and why. From these inputs, we'll construct a flow that connects the dots into a simple, direct, visual of the business—all unified by a single theme."

"Rob, I'd like you to cover the marketing strategy pieces," Sam added. "Dave, you're responsible for digging into the executional excellence components."

"Do you have examples of previous business reviews so we can see what the final product looks like?" Lincoln asked.

"Definitely, Lincoln," Alicia confirmed. "I'll shoot them over right after this meeting."

The room got quiet for a moment and Sam realized everyone was still waiting for him to elaborate on the story. The idea had manifested that morning in the shower, as did a surprising number of his better inspirations.

"Okay," he started. "Now that we know what the executives are expecting, we have a structure for the presentation. We need to cover three main parts: current performance for Induet, emerging gaps, and critical issues. All of you are here because of how I sold senior leadership on the concept of our team, and I think we should stick with this theme. What do you think of *Strength on Strength*?"

He looked around the room to gauge the reaction.

"I like it," Dave chimed in first. "Although it does remind me of some sort of ad slogan for men's deodorant!"

Everyone cracked up. No further critique was raised, so they ratified the theme and got to work.

"For my part," Rob said, "I'll look to elaborate on Harris's perspective on the marketplace, pricing considerations, and product positioning recommendations."

"And we'll demonstrate how we will structure our sales

force and equip the team," Dave added.

"Good," Sam replied. "Lincoln, I'll need you to focus on articulating the strategy to get Goltur covered on all key insurance programs to ensure fast product uptake and a best-in-class launch."

"Got it!" Lincoln agreed.

"Rebecca, I want you riding shotgun with Alicia to learn how we prepare for and build these presentations. You will also run point on liaising with the global Induet team and ensuring alignment with the theme and structure of our presentation. Clear?"

Rebecca held up her hand.

"Yes, Rebecca?"

"Oh, gosh, sorry," she replied. "I wasn't asking a question. That was a five—as in, five for full agreement. We do this thing called *Fist to Five* in the field. When you are fully aligned, you throw up a five. If not, you rate your level of agreement from fist—which is totally unclear or unaligned—all the way up to five."

"Oh yeah, I forgot all about that," Dave said.

"I like that a lot, Rebecca," Sam said. "Fist to Five can help us avoid any miscommunications amongst ourselves. Great stuff!"

Rebecca blushed.

"Now, remember," Sam continued, "most other marketing teams don't put one-tenth of this effort into their reviews. As we go through this rigorous process, you may ask yourselves, 'Why is all this necessary?' Well, it's necessary because a good review buys us credibility, trust, and continued empowerment; a bad review can take those things away. So, please, take this process seriously. Attend all the business review preparation meetings, be fully present in the room, and contribute to the presentation's construction."

With that, they ended the first business review preparation meeting.

Alicia organized five more prep sessions in the five weeks leading up to the formal review. At each meeting, they reviewed the current state of the presentation, examined intelligence on other team reviews, went over the financials again and again until the key points were clearly identified, and decided who would present what and how they would transition between topics and presenters.

For the last two meetings, Sam invited colleagues from supporting departments to sit in, contribute, and provide feedback as well. The final deck ended up progressing through twenty revisions before the big show. On the day of the review, Alicia and Rebecca met with the IT director in the boardroom to set the audio sound levels, review the visibility of the slides from all areas of the room, and test their embedded videos.

Because of the intensity of the process prior to the review and the clear intent to boil everything down to its pure essence, the first review of the Goltur plus Induet marketing team went amazingly smoothly. Everyone hit their marks, and they'd anticipated and prepared for 90 percent of the questions they received. The team got kudos all the way around for a job well done.

The team was buzzing as they emerged victorious from the boardroom. Sam looked around at his group—Rob, Dave, Alicia, Lincoln, and Rebecca alongside their global marketing compatriots Scott Denger (senior director of global marketing), Greg Bundy (director of global market access), and Vignesh Neeru (associate product manager)—extremely proud of their collective effort. They had more than earned a round of celebratory drinks, so Sam invited them to join him at a nearby pub.

Forty-five minutes later, they were all seated underneath a big umbrella at the Black Briar Pub, beers in hand (except for Vignesh, who didn't drink alcohol; he opted for a Coke instead). It was great to be out of the office on such a beautiful day. Sam listened to some of the side conversations and realized that despite the amount of time they had all spent together during the business review preparations, not everyone knew one another well. He made a mental note to schedule a team-building retreat to remedy this situation.

Conversation all but evaporated when Jim arrived a bit later—people noticeably a bit awkward in the presence of the big boss. Jim picked up on the shift and proposed an icebreaker. "Hey, Sam," he said, taking a huge gulp from his pint of Guinness, "how much money would you need to walk away from Giant for good?"

Sam raised his eyebrow, wondering if this was a trap. Why would his boss want to know what it would take for him to leave the company? "That's a tough one to answer, Jim. I've been at Giant for twenty years—can't really put a price on what it would take for me to exit."

"Thanks for the politically correct answer, Sam," Jim said, laughing. "Okay, I'll go first. I used to have my own company and sold it for a nice sum, so this is a bit of an unfair question for me…but my number is roughly the value of my stock options, at a strike price of forty dollars."

Sam did a quick calculation, estimating his boss's stock options to be in the one-million-dollar range. "So around forty million would do it, Jim?"

Jim was impressed. "Not bad, Sam. Now, give us your real answer."

Sam took a swig of beer, aware that all eyes were on him now. "Well, I want to pay off the house, put Michael through college, and have about three hundred thousand a year net for the rest of my life, so, let's do the math. I guess twenty million would cover it."

One by one they took turns naming their price, and Sam realized what Jim had done. By getting everyone to think about their "number," Jim had made each person consider what they were really working for. These areas of importance that Jim, and now Sam, had identified in everyone could be used to calibrate each person's happiness with their job. It was ingenious. The numbers ranged from five to fifty million dollars, except for Lincoln, who claimed he would need a whopping hundred million to leave.

"My rationale is that the value of money keeps declining, and will keep doing so as I get older, so I will need a lot more of it to know that my family and I are fully comfortable for a few lifetimes!"

Sam had to admit that Smarty Pants (as Dave had nicknamed Lincoln) had a point.

With the ice officially broken, conversation flowed more naturally. Until Alicia asked Jim what he'd done with all the money he'd made in the Jade Pharmaceuticals sale and why was he still working.

Sam wanted to slap his forehead in frustration, but Jim was more than willing to answer.

"I was wondering if one of you would ask me about that," Jim said with a smile. "It's the natural question, right? Well, I fully agree with Lincoln here, but I'm a bit more extreme. When I sold Jade, the first thing I did was buy a substantial amount of gold bars as insurance against any unforeseen economic calamity. The rest of the money is invested in different holdings—commodities, currency, capital markets, and corporations. Those are my four Cs of investing. Each hedges against the other over the long term—several lifetimes if it all works out. As to the question about why I am still working, it's simple, really. Loyalty. A long time ago, our new CEO Myra Khan hired an untested and unproven South African kid right out of college and gave me my first shot. She taught me everything I know about the pharma industry, marketing, and business. She was one of the principal investors in Jade. Not only do I respect her, I owe her. I told her that if she ever needed me, I would be there."

Sam was dumbfounded by Jim's response. It told him a lot about his boss—what he valued and how he worked. His disclosure also represented a rare moment of vulnerability, and Sam felt his trust for the man take a leap.

"What I observed today," Jim continued after finishing his pint, "was a team being born. Each of you had each other's backs in there. That type of cohesiveness is difficult to create and even more difficult to break. We are climbing Mt. Everest with this launch, and with this *esprit de corps*, I have no doubt we will be massively successful. So, let's raise our glasses in honor of the man who got us here—Coach!"

Having gone from dumbfounded to flabbergasted, Sam raised his glass as the team drank in his honor.

During the drive home, Sam realized that he would run through walls to keep Jim Kelly happy. He couldn't remember the last time he'd felt that way about a boss. He thought about "the Law of the Lid" from another of John C. Maxwell's classics, ***The 21 Irrefutable Laws of Leadership***. The Law of the Lid basically stated that there was a direct relationship between one's leadership skills (their "lid") and one's overall impact regardless of their efforts to succeed. In this way, a leader with level-three skills could only deliver impact on a level of two or below, whereas a leader with level-ten skills could deliver impact on a nine level—exponentially higher than the level-three leader. The act of improving and increasing one's leadership skills (raising the lid) was a conscious effort to increase leadership capability and doing this dramatically increased one's effectiveness.

Another positive side effect of raising the lid of leadership ability was the increased capacity to influence leaders. In the long term, a leader could only effectively influence those with lower leadership capabilities than he or she possessed. To build a truly high-performing team, leaders needed to develop their own capabilities so they could attract and lead more talented colleagues.

Sam had long been managed by persons less capable as managers than himself. Jim Kelly changed all that. Sam had finally met someone he could learn a lot from, and in turn he could pass these lessons on to his team, creating a virtuous circle.

Jim would raise all their lids and lead them to deliver a world-class launch.

CHAPTER SIX:

STAR SEARCH

Storming – Nine months to launch

A month after the business review, Sam was conducting his weekly staff meeting for the first time with a full team.

"Alright everyone, before we get started, I'd like to introduce our new Market Access Manager, Marcus Gleeson. Marcus is a recent ELITE graduate who's done stints in global marketing, government affairs, and pricing. He went to Cornell, whose mascot is the Big Red Bear. Dave, can you please lead us in welcoming Marcus?"

Ever since the team had bonded over drinks after the business review, they'd gotten a lot closer. Every day they went to lunch as a team and had taken to calling each other nicknames. Alicia became Striker (she'd graduated from Florida A&M, the Rattlers); Lincoln remained Smarty Pants; Sam was Coach; Dave was CC for Comedy Central (he was funny 24/7); Rob was AC or Assassin's Creed (due to his ninja-like strategic skills and cool demeanor); and Rebecca was Bulldog (she'd graduated from the University of Georgia). Jim Kelly was, of course, Churchill (just not to his face).

"Welcome to the team, Marcus," Dave opened. "I took the liberty of digging into your background a bit to figure out what to call you, but nothing beats your college mascot. So, I hereby christen you Huggy Bear!"

"Hey, Huggy," Alicia greeted.

"Welcome aboard, HB," Lincoln said.

"Welcome to the team, Mr. Bear," Rob echoed.

"Okay," Sam said, "why don't you tell us a bit more about yourself, Hugs?"

Sam studied Marcus to see if he'd fit in or not. They were building a culture here, and the nicknames were a part of it, just like the dart board in Dave's office or the Rubik's Cube passed on to the colleague with the most innovative ideas each month. During his interview, Marcus had established himself as strongest in the **W**ork Ethic and **H**eart elements of Sam's **W.H.O.M.** This was his chance to demonstrate his attitude, maturity, and flexibility.

"Thanks for the warm welcome, all," Marcus started. "Now that you mention it, our mascot is quite huggable, as am I! Anyway, I'm from Westville, a small town in upstate New York, where I grew up the middle of three boys. I'm six months married, and my wife is expecting our first child right after we deliver the greatest launch in the history of the category. Very happy to work with and learn from you all."

His response elicited spontaneous applause from the team and a subtle head nod from Dave to Sam—they'd gotten another one right. The next step was to transform this high engagement level into equally high productivity. Rob was focused on the strategic interfaces with Harris: market research, direct-to-consumer advertising, digital marketing and promotions, product positioning, and pricing. Lincoln was concentrating on key opinion-leader engagement while Marcus would tackle pricing and access.

Dave led Giant's executional efforts: sales force effectiveness, performance analytics, internal communications, and promotional medical education. His team was rounded out with Rebecca on communications and Alicia taking the lead on promotional medical education and vendor management. They were a young and hungry bunch, and soon Sam noticed an emerging pattern.

Every Monday during the staff meeting, Sam would rattle off a list of strategic or executional tasks. His expectation was that Rob and Dave, as team leaders, would sort out who was doing what. It soon became apparent, however, that Alicia, Marcus, Lincoln, and Rebecca were in a competition of sorts to take on Sam's tasks and see who could outdo the others. While the can-do spirit was admirable, the competition was quite counterproductive.

Things came to a head when Rebecca marched into Sam's office one afternoon to complain about what was going on behind the scenes. Rebecca, an ER doctor before migrating into pharma sales, was not easily rattled. If she was upset, something must be wrong. Sam knew the trouble brewing needed his prompt attention.

"What's going on, Bulldog?"

"Coach, I can't work like this. The disorganization and chaos are off the charts with all these competing priorities. People are not being held accountable as they should."

"What do you mean?"

"I was tasked this week with sending a field bulletin on the new promotional resources for Induet. My plan was to send it out on Wednesday, but when I asked Lincoln for the feedback from our physician advisory board, which I wanted to include, he informed me that he didn't have it done yet. Apparently, he's been focusing on the update to our promotional slide kit."

"Why is Lincoln working on that? That's Alicia's area," Sam replied.

"Exactly! I went to Alicia to see if she could take the slide kit from Lincoln's hands so he could get back on the advisory board comments, and she mentioned that she was swamped trying to get the latest market research questionnaire approved through medical/legal review. When I asked her why she was working on the questionnaire, when that was Lincoln's responsibility, she said that she was just doing what you'd asked her to do."

Sam was troubled by Rebecca's report. "Okay, Rebecca. Thanks for letting me know. I'll fix it."

Sam immediately called a meeting with Dave and Rob to see how they could facilitate better workplace communication and get the team running like a well-oiled machine. They tried several strategies, such as being more explicit in job assignments, but nothing was working. Despite the clear role definitions, some people were naturally inclined toward another person's tasks, which led them to encroach on their teammate's territory. Unfortunately, everyone's good intentions were negatively impacting productivity.

They needed an intervention.

Sam called Missy Richards, a team-building consultant and professional coach he'd worked with in the past. He explained the issue and solicited her advice.

"Doesn't sound like you're playing to your people's natural strengths, Sam," she said. "But fret not, I've got just the program you need."

Two days later, she sent over a proposal. She was offering a full-day workshop on individual and team strength identification based on a book and assessment created by Donald O. Clifton and the Gallup organization called *StrengthsFinder 2.0* and the **Clifton Strengths® Assessment**, respectively. She included a copy of the book with the proposal and encouraged Sam to read the first four chapters and take the assessment himself before confirming the workshop.

Sam took the book home with him over the weekend. In between completing Patricia's "honey-do" list and shooting some hoops with Michael, he read the whole thing. Sam was intrigued by the theory that the key to productivity was to develop natural talents into strengths. Western education and corporate norms were based on developing weaknesses, not strengths.

The basic idea was to identify one's unique talents, accept them, and then sharpen, develop, and apply them until they became reliable strengths. A weakness was either a "lesser talent" *or* a dominant talent that was not being productively applied and which might be adversely impacting both the individual and others.

Sam thought back on his own life and wondered what he might have achieved if someone had identified his gifted areas at a young age and then deliberately helped him develop these gifts. He'd spent years—first in school and later in the workplace—trying to be better at things he didn't do well. His organizing habits were a great example.

Over the years, boss after boss had encouraged him to be more organized. Some had even incorporated performance measures into his development plans based on his demonstration of improved organizational capabilities. Still, the mess always won the day. He'd invested tons of time and energy attempting to develop an area of natural weakness. Gallup was offering a different approach, and his curiosity was piqued. First thing Sunday morning, he poured himself a cup of coffee and sat down to take the assessment.

Forty-five minutes later he was done, and he received an email detailing his top five "signature" talent themes. Themes were the collation of similar traits into a singular designation. Apparently, there were thirty-four unique talent themes in total. The order of the themes mattered in that the top five were considered the dominant themes and likely to be more prevalent in daily life. Sam read the report with keen interest.

His signature themes were Communication, Maximizer, Self-Assurance, Learner, and Developer . Communication refers to persons with the ability to translate concepts into a form that could be understood by others, whether that be through conversations, presentations, or writing. A Maximizer is to someone who strengthens and improves group perfor-mance by encouraging both individual members and the group as a whole to aspire to excellence. One who excels in Self-Assurance inspires confidence in other people by working through difficult and uncertain situations. Those who are considered Learners are dedicated to learning and therefore continually work on improving their performance, while Developers enjoy cultivating such potential in others.

A funny thing started to happen to Sam as he read about his talents—he started feeling special and unique. He was energized by these ideas and wanted to understand more (perhaps that was his Learner side coming out). A whole new world of possibilities emerged, and Sam now understood why the Clifton Strengths® approach formed the basis of Missy's recommendation. It was some seriously powerful stuff!

Over dinner that evening he introduced the concept to Patricia and Michael, and they were very much into it. They agreed with the results of his assessment and gave him concrete examples of times he'd exhibited behaviors related to his signature themes. Sam ordered enough books for his team and one each for Patricia and Michael). Then he emailed Missy to confirm that, yes, he wanted her to conduct the workshop.

Two weeks later, the whole team convened at the Short Hills Hilton in a well-appointed conference room. Missy opened the session with an icebreaker exercise called Fact vs. Fiction. Each person was asked to write down three statements about themselves on a Post-it—two false and one true—and tack it to the wall. Then everyone tried to guess fiction from fact.

Who would have imagined that Rob had once climbed Mt. Kilimanjaro, or that Alicia had skydived over fifty times? Even though the team worked very closely together every day, there was still much they didn't know about one another. Missy explained that the day's session was designed to enhance their knowledge of themselves and their teammates to drive greater cohesiveness, engagement, and productivity.

Next, they discussed the Clifton Strengths® philosophy, the thirty-four talent themes, and transforming talent into strength. Missy asked everyone to share their opinions of the book and the results of their assessments. Sam could feel the buzz in the room as they revealed their thoughts about the overall philosophy and their individual results. He did notice a bit of a generational gap in terms of initial acceptance; Rob and Dave remained quite skeptical while their direct reports were all-in.

Conferring with Missy during the morning break, he asked, "How damaging is it to our strengths journey if Rob and Dave don't buy in and apply it?"

"When managers don't apply the science to developing their people, the whole process can collapse," she replied. "Although some very resilient people can persist and improve despite leadership buy-in, it's quite difficult and not a common occurrence in my experience. I recently worked with a client who rolled Clifton Strengths® out at an enterprise level— meaning every single person in the company took the assessment and received their top-five reports, and several training interventions were activated for the line managers to effectively coach based on strengths. Unfortunately, the CEO was unable to secure full buy-in from some strong dissenters on his leadership team who ultimately derailed the success of the overall effort. My point being that to get the most out of the system, your senior-most leaders need to believe in it and drive it."

"Hmm. Well, we are not forcing anyone to change their lives based on this. Still, how do I encourage Rob and Dave to open their minds more to the idea?" Sam asked.

"If you begin to consistently apply the science with them, it will go a long way. We can arrange for in-depth coaching sessions with a Gallup-certified strengths coach as well."

Sam agreed and had Missy set it up. Rob and Dave seemed receptive, but Sam knew that embedding this approach would be easier said than done.

The truly revelatory part of the day came when Missy introduced the concept of the "Four Domains of Strength" in which all thirty-four talent themes were grouped. The domains were: Strategic Thinking, Relationship Building, Influencing, and Execution. *Strategic Thinking* referred to the ability to absorb and analyze information to improve decision-making; *Relationship Building* referred to the ability to build strong relationships and generate synergies; *Influencing* referred to the ability to take charge, speak up, and be heard; and *Executing* referred to the ability to make things happen.

"This grid is the DNA of this team," she said, providing them with a handout entitled "Team DNA – US Goltur/Induet Cholesterol-Management Team."

Team Members	Achiever®	Arranger®	Belief®	Consistency®	Deliberate®	Discipline®	Focus®	Responsibility®	Restorative®	Activator®	Command®	Communication®	Competition®	Maximizer®	Self-Assurance®	Significance®	Woo®	Adaptability®	Connectedness®	Developer®	Empathy®	Harmony®	Includer®	Individualization®	Positivity®	Relator®	Analytical®	Context®	Futuristic®	Ideation®	Input®	Intellection®	Learner®	Strategic®
(Domain)	Execution									Influence								Relationship Building									Strategic Thinking							
Theme Rank	2							1					4	5																				3
Sam												1	2	3						5													4	
Rob					5																			4			1	2						3
Dave	1													3	2								4							5				
Lincoln	5							4																					2			3		1
Marcus	2							4	3				1			5																		
Alicia								5			3				4															1				2
Gaile								4											3		2	1				5								
Rebecca	2							1					4	3										5										
Count	4	0	0	0	1	0	0	5	1	0	1	1	3	3	2	1	0	0	1	1	1	1	1	2	0	1	1	1	1	2	0	1	1	3
Total	10	0	0	0	5	0	0	18	3	0	3	1	7	9	6	5	0	0	3	5	2	1	4	9	0	5	1	2	2	6	0	3	4	6
Talent Coverage	44%									75%								78%									88%							
Talent Concentration	15%									17%								11%									16%							

"This chart contains a wealth of information, so let me walk you through it," Missy said. "The top two rows show you which talent themes cluster into which strength domains. There are *nine* Execution and Relationship-Building talents and *eight* Influence and Strategic-Thinking talents. If you look at the row labeled *Count*, you can see that this team covers twenty-four of thirty-four talent themes or seventy-one percent of the total. Are you following?"

Everyone nodded.

"Good. Now, let's look at each team member's talent mapping. You will notice that the color-coding of the team members is aligned with dominance in a specific domain. This gives us our first key insight into the team dynamic. As you can see, your leading team members in Strategic Thinking are Rob, Lincoln, and Alicia. Your strongest team member in Relationship Building is Gaile. Your dominant Influencers are Sam and Dave. And Rebecca and Marcus are the most prominent in Execution."

"Wait, Missy," Alicia said. "There are many of us with multiple talents in Influence, but you've mapped us as dominant in a different domain. Why is that?"

"Anyone want to hazard a guess?" Missy replied.

Lincoln spoke up. "Because our talents are ranked in order of dominance, so the lower the sum of the talent ranking in a domain, the higher the potential dominance?"

"Very good, Lincoln!" Missy said. "In your case, Alicia, your third and fourth talents are mapped to Influence and your first and second are in Strategic Thinking. So, to Lincoln's point, three is more dominant than seven."

Understanding dawned on Alicia's face.

"This is too much math, Missy!" Dave interjected. "Can you make it simpler?"

"I know this takes a bit to digest, Dave, but please bear with me, okay? There are three other key pieces of information here. Look at row three—Theme Rank—and the bottom two rows—Talent Coverage and Talent Concentration. Theme Rank tells you the themes that rise as most dominant among the team in order of prominence. Talent Coverage simply means the number of total talents present for this team in each domain and helps you identify any potential blind spots, like the ten themes missing from this team, and helps you understand the impact of their absence. Talent Concentration goes a step further by showing how deep the team is in each of the four domains. If I only looked at Theme Rank, I would say this team is dominant in Execution and Influence, but when I layer in Talent Concentration and Talent Coverage, I see a lack of breadth in Execution, or how this team gets things done, whereas there is good depth and breadth of talents in Influence and Strategic Thinking. That means there is a lot of variety in how the team can solve problems and advocate for itself. And by all measures, this team has a big potential blind spot in Relationship Building. Did I lose you?"

Sam's brain was on fire as he started connecting dots he hadn't even known were present. "I'm right with you, Missy, and this is amazingly insightful!" he said to positive head nods from his team.

Missy then reviewed the areas where the team had the highest potential talent. The team's top five signature talent themes were Responsibility (with five team members possessing this talent), Achiever (four members), Strategic (three members), Competition (three members), and Maximizer (three members). She provided an overview of the characteristics of each of these themes for team application.

Responsibility® X 5 (Execution)	Teams strong in the Responsibility theme **take psychological ownership of what they say they will do.** They are committed to stable values such as honesty and loyalty.
Achiever® X 4 (Execution)	Teams strong in the Achiever theme have a great deal of stamina and **work hard.** They take great satisfaction from being busy and productive.
Strategic® X 3 (Strategic Thinking)	Teams exceptionally talented in the Strategic theme create alternative ways to proceed. Faced with any given scenario, they can **quickly spot the relevant patterns and issues.**
Competition® X 3 (Influencing)	Teams exceptionally talented in the Competition theme measure their progress against the performance of others. They **strive to win first place** and revel in contests.
Maximizer® X 3 (Influencing)	Teams exceptionally talented in the Maximizer theme **focus on strengths as a way to stimulate personal and group excellence.** They seek to transform something strong into something superb.

"Once again, this team is more Execution and Influence dominant due to having two Execution themes and two Influencing themes in the top five," she said. "I'd like you to pair up and answer the following questions so we can delve a bit deeper."

She clicked to a slide with a list of seven questions:

1. What are the patterns of behavior that result from our team's top talent themes?
2. How do we communicate?
3. What drives us?"
4. How do we set direction and make decisions?
5. How do we overcome obstacles?
6. How do we build and maintain relationships?
7. How do we recognize each other and celebrate success?

Sam paired off with Marcus, and they worked through the questions. After ten minutes, Missy led them through a debrief. She started with Alicia and Rob and finished with Sam and Marcus, compiling the collective themes as each group spoke. The final product was then revealed.

1. What are the patterns of behavior that result from our team's top talent themes?
   - *Hard work, commitment, productivity, high drive, and continuous improvement.*

2. How do we communicate?
   - *Straight to the point, highly transparent, rapid-fire,*

clear expectations.

3. What drives us?
   - *Winning, completion of tasks, raising the bar, and excellence.*

4. How do we set direction and make decisions?
   - *Consider options collaboratively, then align and execute.*

5. How do we overcome obstacles?
   - *Brute force combined with strategizing.*

6. How do we build and maintain relationships?
   - *Group lunches, darts in Dave's office.*

7. How do we recognize each other and celebrate success?
   - *Beers at Black Briar Pub after business reviews.*

"Hopefully, now you have a deeper understanding of what makes this team tick. But it's not all rainbows and unicorns. Inherent in each theme is an upside and downside." She advanced to a new slide entitled "Balconies and Basements."

Theme	Balcony (Brand builder)	Basement (Barrier to success)
Achiever® X 5 (Execution)	Tireless, strong work ethic, leads by example, go-getter, hungry	Unbalanced, overcommitted, can't say no, burns the candle at both ends, too concentrated on work, work is more important than people
Responsibility® X 4 (Execution)	Committed, accountable, independent, trusted, conscientious	Micromanager, obsessive, can't say no, takes on too much
Strategic® X 3 (Strategic Thinking)	Anticipates alternatives, intuitive, sees different paths	Jumps to quick decisions, difficult to understand his or her thinking, close-minded
Competition® X 3 (Influencing)	Driven, motivated, number one, measurement oriented, winner	Sore loser, not team players, puts down others, self-centered, confrontational
Maximizer® X 3 (Influencing)	Mastery, success, excellence, enjoys working with the best	Perfectionist, picky, never good enough, always reworking

"I see some of you cringing at the basement side of this chart, which I take to mean you see yourself reflected somewhat there. The fact is, you can either leverage your dominant talents to build a powerful brand inside of your company and in the industry, or you can become derailed by the negative aspects of these same themes. It takes concerted effort and constant feedback to remain in your balcony state. High-performance teams remain committed to driving excellence by actively minimizing their basements. What, if any, patterns can you detect within the team based on this information?"

"Well, to me it seems we as a team have a bias toward action, which is great," Rob commented. "However, we could probably benefit from taking a step back and making sure we are all coordinated and joined up before jumping into execution."

"Totally agree, Rob," Marcus joined in. "I'm also a bit concerned about our high competition aspect. I think it's productive if focused at winning versus the outside world, but if we start competing amongst ourselves, then we will likely get less done, which will frustrate our executional efforts."

"Any other observations?" Missy probed.

"Well," Lincoln ventured, "we clearly have a high commitment and work capacity—so the intention seems to be in the right place. But reflecting on myself, I've got no relationship-building talents in my top five, and neither does our team. How do we make sure we stay together and not allow our task orientation to disrupt productive working relationships? I think this will be a key area to focus on."

Sam now understood why his people kept tripping over themselves to get projects done. Due to the high Responsibility and Achiever aspects of his team, people were jumping into action before effectively coordinating and aligning. And the Competition aspect didn't help, to Marcus's point. It wasn't enough to be explicit about who was doing what; they would *also* need to link the work to their strengths and harness their powerful collective talents while keeping their relationship-building blind spot top of mind.

"Everything makes so much more sense now," Rebecca commented as several team members nodded their heads in agreement. "We've got some work to do!"

"Every team that wants to perform at the highest level

does, Rebecca," Missy replied. "The key is for each of you to reflect on your individual talents and assess the degree to which you use them for the good of the team. You have a natural blind spot in relationship building and should probably lean more on Gaile, who has four talents in this area."

After a break, Missy transitioned into a workshop focused on creating a sustainable team culture. As pre-work for the final session, Missy had each colleague complete a thirty-seven-question assessment on team dynamics and cultural attributes. The questions were rated two ways—first by level of satisfaction, and next according to level of importance.

"Each question was related to a specific high-performing team attribute," Missy explained. "From the responses you gave, I was able to assess proficiency in a given category. I then compiled these results so we can use them to better understand the team's values, trust level, cohesiveness, and overall effectiveness. Okay?"

Sam noted the nods of understanding from around the table. "Sounds good," he said.

"This table here," she said, advancing the slide, "depicts the top six questions ranked in order of importance."

Q #	Category	Level of Satisfaction	Level of Importance	Proficiency score
18	**Trust** The trust, respect and sensitivity we show to one another by actively listening to and appropriately validating one another's perspectives	7.29	8.86	82%
3	**Shared Values** The extent to which our team has shared core values that are clear and unambiguous, and appropriately guide our behavior and priorities	6.86	8.86	77%
1	**Mission/Purpose** The mission/purpose of the team and the extent to which it inspires us to work effectively together	8.29	8.71	95%
4	**Productive Conflict** The balance of time we spend as a team on tasks, i.e. getting things done, versus doing what is needed to build cohesiveness of the team, e.g., resolving conflict, clarifying our purpose or goals, and ensuring everyone gets heard	6.71	8.71	77%
6	**Commitment** Our ability to end discussions with clear and specific resolutions and calls to action	6.71	8.71	77%
7	**Accountability** My role on the team, (as opposed to your job role), and the clarity of my team members' expectations of me in that capacity	6.29	8.71	72%

"What do you see?" she inquired.

Alicia dove in first. "Well, if I'm reading this right, in most of the areas that are most important to us as a team, we are pretty average in satisfying those needs."

"And," Dave chipped in, "I don't trust *any* of you fools!"

The group cracked up.

"Speaking seriously, team values and trust are the foundation for effective relationships," Missy explained. "And the bottom line of trust is a willingness to be vulnerable." Heads nodded around the room as she put up a slide. "This team's self-score on Trust is pretty average: eighty-two percent."

She clicked and two bullets were revealed:

- *Question #18: The trust, respect and sensitivity we show to one another by actively listening to and appropriately validating one another's perspectives (7.29 satisfaction/8.86 importance) = 82 percent proficiency.*
- *Question #3: The extent to which we have shared core values that are clear and unambiguous, and appropriately guide our behavior (6.86 satisfaction/8.86 importance) = 77 percent proficiency.*

"So, yes, there are several gaps to be addressed in your goal to become a high-performing team. My advice, based on these results, is to start with trust."

"Why trust?" Lincoln asked. "Looks like accountability is the lowest item on the list."

"Because the level of importance to the team is higher, right, Missy?" Marcus interjected.

"Bingo," Missy confirmed.

The workshop ended on that note, but Sam knew it was just the beginning of a long journey toward excellence for him and his team. He thanked Missy for her time and insight and looked forward to putting this new knowledge into practice.

Sam took the group out to dinner at a nearby restaurant and was pleased to hear them applying the new language of talent they'd just learned.

"So, guys and gals, what's your feedback on the day? What was your biggest takeaway?" he asked.

"My takeaway is that you people are weird," Dave replied, laughing. "I mean, who masters the harmonica, Rebecca? Really?"

Everyone laughed.

"No, seriously," Dave continued, "the more I get to know everyone's strengths—I mean, *talent themes*—the more convinced I am that we can do something special. But you influencers gotta stay outta my head! I'm warning you!"

Marcus laughed. "This was my first time going through something like this, and I just want to thank Sam for giving us the opportunity to bond and get to know each other, and ourselves, better. As the newest member of the team, I feel like I'm fully immersed now and ready to work!"

"Hear, hear," Alicia said. "But we should start addressing some of the underdeveloped areas Missy revealed from the assessment, too."

Sam nodded in agreement. "Definitely, Alicia. We will start working on this as soon as we get back to the office. And your take, Rob?"

"You all know I am a natural skeptic," Rob replied in his deliberate manner. "But I know truth when I experience it, and I believe that there is something to this strengths-based science. I can't argue with the culture- and values-assessment results. I just need to understand better how to apply this in our day-to-day, and I know that will take some work on my part, but I'm committed to try."

Sam smiled. They were officially on the right path.

CHAPTER SEVEN:
BASIC BRILLIANCE

Storming – Eight months to launch

Despite the energizing Clifton Strengths® workshop and initial enthusiasm for its principles, little had changed around the office. Missy had warned Sam that he needed to stop seeing roles and start seeing people, but it was very difficult to adjust his own expectations of the work a colleague should be doing. Sam realized he needed even more help, so he decided to reach out to one of his mentors, Logan Dunn. Logan, the former president of Giant, was currently head of the leadership consultancy, Dunn Strategists.

Logan was the leader who'd bet on Sam early in his career by shifting him from PR into a career in marketing. Logan had mentored Sam all the way to senior marketing director before leaving Giant during the leadership transition.

Sam waited patiently for Logan's admin to patch the call through.

"Sam! Great to hear from you," Logan said when he picked up the line.

"I know—long time no speak. How's life on the other side?"

"I'm thriving! Loving this consulting lifestyle. Truth be told, I should have made this move years earlier!"

"Glad to hear everything's going great. We missed you at the game last week," Sam replied, referencing the Rutgers versus Virginia Tech basketball game. "You missed a battle! Lance Parker had a beast of a game—twenty-six points, eight assists, twelve boards, and five blocks!"

"Don't remind me," Logan said. "The wife was sick, so I stayed home to tend to her."

"Sorry to hear that," Sam said. "How is Maggie doing?"

"Much better now, thanks. Almost done with the chemo, which has been the hardest part. But the prognosis is good, and she's been an absolute trouper. We're very fortunate to have caught the cancer early."

"Sounds like she's on the road to recovery. That's one special lady you've got over there. Please send her my love."

"Of course, Sam," Logan replied. "How are things on your end?"

"Pretty good, Logan. Pretty good. We're eight months out from a new product launch, and I've got a nice team assembled. The right **W.H.O.M.** is in place. But I'm still struggling with optimizing productivity. That's why I'm calling. You're the best team builder I know, and I could use your advice."

"Okay then," Logan said. "Why don't you tell me more about your team?"

Sam reviewed his people one by one, including their backgrounds, **W.H.O.M.** interview assessments, signature talent themes, and gaps. As he introduced each colleague, Logan peppered him with questions, like: "What drives him or her?"

"Were they an only child?" "What do or did their parents do for work?"

Once Sam finished discussing Marcus Gleeson, he concluded with, "So, that's the team. What do you think?"

Logan took a moment to collect his thoughts. "Well, a couple of things stand out for me, and the first is one I see all the time. I don't get the sense that you really know these people. A few spare facts and interesting tidbits, yes, but if you want to create a truly high-performance team, you are going to have to dig a bit deeper, my friend."

Sam was taken aback. "How can you say that, Logan? I feel like I've got a great handle on my people."

"All leaders do," Logan countered. "Tell me this: Alicia Barden—why did she attend a historically black university?"

Sam opened his mouth to respond, but then had to admit, "I don't know. But why is that relevant to getting her to produce in the here and now?"

"I'll explain in a moment," Logan said. "You know I was in the Army, right?"

"Yes."

"Well, in the military, before the troops get down to specializing and mission planning, they all have to go through the same standard process."

"Boot camp?" Sam asked.

"Yes. Or Basic, as we call it," Logan replied. "And why does this process exist?"

"Well, I don't come from a military background, but my assumption is that what the military wants is to turn heterogeneous groups of people into homogenous groups. Once homogeneity is achieved, then work can progress in a standard way. Boot camp—I mean Basic—is the mechanism to achieve this."

"Okay, but why?" Logan asked.

Sam thought about it. "I have no idea."

"You might be surprised to learn that Basic arose in the US as a strategy to rehabilitate and reform soldiers who committed crimes during World War II and the post-war period."

Sam *was* surprised. "Basic training was designed as a punishment mechanism?"

"Originally, yes. But the results allowed forty-two thousand soldiers to return to active duty. It was only then that the US Army understood what they had—a conditioning program to prepare soldiers' bodies and minds for the rigors of combat. The key to the recipe lay in a steady diet of escalating physical challenges and submission to total control. By the time a cadet passed through Basic, they were fully indoctrinated into military culture, from the respect for the chain of command and taking orders to the various specific ways to do everything from making beds and cleaning guns to planning and executing missions. The indoctrinated then passed the culture down the line to successive groups. From there, the culture drove performance."

"So, you think my team lacks a clear culture?" Sam asked.

"Bingo. You have excited people with the strengths philosophy, which is a good start, but what happens if someone doesn't adhere to it? The nicknames are good, but are they superficial or is there deeper understanding of the individual that comes with the shorthand? And why don't you—the leader—know the building blocks of your people's stories so you can link them back to both your team's culture and the company's culture?"

Sam bristled at the criticism. Why was his friend and mentor attacking him?

"Listen, Sam, I'm sorry for being so blunt, but you asked for help, right?"

"Well, yes," Sam replied hesitantly.

"This is what help looks like. I am a big mirror reflecting your actions, and lack thereof, back at you. If you don't like what you see, then maybe you should consider making some changes to your approach."

Sam knew Logan was right, but damn did the feedback sting. "Okay, so I don't have a high-performance team culture. Where do you recommend I start?"

"When you join the military or really *any* high-performance organization," Logan replied, "the culture smacks you in the face because it is reinforced by everything you do and everyone you meet. It becomes the unquestionable *why*, *how*, and *what* of your organizational existence. It makes everything easier for everyone because it removes any ambiguity in terms of purpose, strategy, and key goals. Right now, Giant's corporate culture is unsteady because of the new management. So, you can either wait for the senior execs to define it for you, or you can manifest your own by getting to know your people on an elemental level. Take the question I asked about Alicia. What if the reason she went to an all-black university was driven by her trying to better discover her own cultural identity? To the extent that this is important to her, if you ignore it, you may miss out on a powerful environmental motivator related to her esteem—and missing this may lead to her performance not being fully maximized. Make sense? In any event, I am running into another meeting now. Please stay in touch and let me know how it goes. And please give my best to Patricia and Michael."

They said their good-byes, and then Sam was left alone with his perturbed thoughts. *Where did I go wrong?* He'd carefully chosen each team member with the **W.H.O.M.** process and then forced them to collaborate due to the robust business review system and even taken them to an offsite team-building workshop on team talent and strengths. Each colleague had a nickname and enjoyed working with the other colleagues. This was all good, wasn't it? So why wasn't he seeing results?

Sam *hoped* everything would come together, but hope was not a strategy. Meanwhile, basic training had a sixty-year track record of taking individuals from all walks of life and turning them into expert soldiers and finely tuned teams driven to complete any mission placed before them. The same could be said for most successful companies—they came with a palpable culture. How could he build something similar while remaining aligned to Giant's core values?

Realizing he wasn't going to solve the problem by himself, he called a meeting with Rob and Dave to discuss the challenge.

He laid out the problem. "We have a working understanding of each other, share similar traits, and appear to enjoy working together, but that alone won't guarantee breakout performance, will it?"

"Never has, in my experience," Rob replied.

Dave nodded in agreement.

"So, what's the next step?" Sam asked. "How do we coalesce these players into a masterful orchestra?"

"Well, Giant's core values are a clear starting point for cultural alignment," Rob started, "but in my experience team culture cannot be imposed on a group. It should arise organically *because* of the people involved. We may know some basic information about our people in terms of what drives their work ethic, motivation, solution orientation, and maturity, but I'm not sure we understand *how* they got this way," Rob declared.

"So, for you the key is in the *how*, not the *what*," Sam clarified. "If that's the case then how do we get them to tell us their *how*?"

"We can do **INNERviews**!" Dave exclaimed.

"We've already done interviews, Dave," Rob replied.

"Not interviews, AC, **INNERviews**! We need to better understand the backstories of our people so we can use that understanding to create an environment where each person can shine. Get it?"

"Makes sense," Rob agreed.

"Good," Sam said, taking charge. "Let's agree to prioritize these **INNERviews** this week, and then come back together

Friday afternoon to construct the culture." Sam stood up, eager to get to work on his new project. "I'll call Missy to see if she has any resources or templates we can use for the dialogues."

Fortunately, Missy had several dialogue tools designed to get to another level of understanding of each colleague; she used them regularly in her coaching sessions to get to know her clients better. "The most important thing," she cautioned, "is to let your colleague know that the conversation is all about them."

Sam set up his initial **INNERview** with Alicia for the following day, allotting an hour for the conversation. Using Missy's discussion guide as the backdrop for the dialogue, he aimed to set the right tone before they got started.

"Hi, Alicia, thanks for making the time for this chat," he began. "Today is all about you. I realized that we still don't know a lot about each other, and this conversation will hopefully go a long way in solving that problem."

"Okay…" Alicia replied.

Sam launched right in. "So, is there another name you prefer being called, other than Alicia or Striker?"

"Not really, I'm fine with either," she replied. Then she suddenly offered, "But my friends back in school called me Stockton because of my basketball-passing skills."

"Oh wow. That's a perfect nickname as well!" Sam exclaimed. He decided to take a leap and ask Alicia the question that Logan had asked him. "Speaking of your time in college, why did you choose to attend FAMU versus some other institution? I'm sure you had many options."

"Oh, I did," Alicia replied. "But FAMU was the only school that offered me a full five-year scholarship *and* the opportunity to play on the basketball team. I was a very good high school player, but I was probably the third best player on my squad and didn't get much recruitment love. Until FAMU came along, that is. My Dad and I took a trip to campus, and I met the coach. She was quite excited about having me, so I made the decision on the spot to go there. And it was the right choice for me! I got to pursue my passion while getting a fantastic education at the same time."

"That's quite interesting and tells me a lot about what was motivating you at the time," Sam said. "Was it a similar process that got you to join Giant?"

"I think we've discussed this before, Sam, but I am here at Giant primarily because of your friend Chuck Towns. He's been recruiting for Giant from FAMU for many years, and we developed a rapport. He let me know that Giant was serious about two topics—diversity and talent development—and basically convinced me that it would be a huge mistake to go anywhere else."

"Okay, so is it safe to say then that relationships are key to gaining your trust, and being allowed to pursue your passions is a key motivational factor?"

"Definitely," she replied. "I like having the freedom to innovate and make course corrections, and both FAMU and Giant are environments where I've been allowed to express my unique creativity and strategic abilities."

Sam furiously took notes as the **INNERview** progressed

deeper. Alicia was quite open, and Sam advanced through the discussion guide, asking her:

1. When is your birthday? Are birthdays important to you?
2. Tell me more about your family background. What do your parents do for work? How many siblings do you have? What do they do?
3. What were some key turning points in your life that made you the person you are today?
4. What do you really love about your work?
5. What drives you crazy about your work?
6. Did you expect to be doing this kind work at this time in your life?
7. What attributes do you value in your best friends?
8. What has been the highlight of your life so far?
9. What do you most regret about your life?
10. How do you want people to view you?
11. When do you feel the most pride about your work?
12. When you achieve success at work, how do you like to be recognized?

Despite having worked with Alicia for over a year, Sam learned a tremendous amount from this conversation. He could tell that Alicia was impressed and touched that he was taking the time to get to know her on a deeper level. And the turning point question evoked a very emotional answer; she cried as she described the impact losing her grandfather at an early age had on her life.

Dave and Rob reported similar experiences after they completed their separate **INNERviews**. They compared notes and developed an outline of key individual motivators, energizers, and recognition preferences across the team. After synthesizing key themes, Dave put the findings into a table for easier examination.

Name	Value Most	Motivators	De-Motivators	Preferred Recognition type
Alicia	Freedom to innovate and freedom to make course corrections	Coming up with something new and finding the path forward	Status quo and passivity	Public and private
Lincoln	Freedom to make course corrections and time to ponder the future	Finding the path forward and taking inspiration from dreaming	Status quo and thoughtlessness	Public
Marcus	Peers for comparison and freedom to work at own pace	Going against the best and completing tasks	Coming in second and lack of diligence	Public
Rebecca	Freedom to take ownership and work at own pace	Respect of others and completing tasks	Disappointing others and lack of diligence	Public
Gaile	Finding common ground and freedom to express emotions	Putting team goals over personal agendas and being a part of the human range of emotions and experiences	Negative friction and things that block or limit emotional expression	Private

"What's highlighted in green and red are the common themes," Dave explained.

They all took a few minutes to digest the information before Rob spoke. "It looks like there are some common de-motivators that we need to watch out for with our team."

"Yeah," Dave replied. "This is a conscientious bunch, and they don't take disappointing others or losing lying down. We have to be extra careful in setting and managing expectations."

"While at the same time making space for creativity and letting them know it's okay to take some risks," Sam interjected. "But this is *gold*, guys! This information tells us who we are as a group and what we value, and helps define our motivators. Imagine…"

"Hold on, Sam," Rob interrupted. "The three of us are not represented in the chart."

"That won't change it that much, will it?"

"Let's see," Dave said, suggesting that each of them add their own values, motivators, de-motivators, and preferred recognition types to the list. Once finished, they studied the results.

Name	Value Most	Motivators	De-motivators	Preferred Recognition type
Alicia	Freedom to innovate and freedom to make course corrections	Coming up with something new and finding the path forward	Status quo and passivity	Public and private
Lincoln	Freedom to make course corrections and time to ponder the future	Finding the path forward and taking inspiration from dreaming	Status quo and thoughtlessness	Public
Marcus	Peers for comparison and freedom to work at own pace	Going against the best and completing tasks	Coming in second and lack of diligence	Public
Rebecca	Freedom to take ownership and work at own pace	Respect of others and completing tasks	Disappointing others and lack of diligence	Public
Gaile	Finding common ground and freedom to express emotions	Putting team goals over personal agendas and being a part of the human range of emotions and experiences	Negative friction and things that block or limit emotional expression	Private
Dave	Freedom to work at own pace and peers for comparison	Completion of tasks and going against the best	Lack of diligence and coming in second	Private
Rob	Time to think and having background information	Data and facts	Things that are not proven and forgetting the past	Private
Sam	Sounding board and quality over quantity focus	Stories and storytellers and maximizing ROI	Experience without expression and obsession with weakness fixing	Public

"Throw in different spices and the dish comes out tasting different," remarked Rob, who knew a thing or two about mixing and matching ingredients due to his love of cooking.

"That's beautiful, Rob," Dave quipped. "Um, Coach. What the hell does 'experience without expression' even mean?"

"Well," Sam said, "I really dislike when I'm not given

the chance to explain a situation clearly. It also bothers me when things can't be put into words or described adequately. It's like a missed opportunity to connect the dots for people when that happens."

"Gotcha," Dave replied, leaning back in his seat. "This is all really interesting, but how do we use this information to build a culture?"

"I've got an idea," Sam said, standing up. On his whiteboard, he drew three columns titled "Why We Exist," "How We Work," and "What We Will Accomplish." Under "Why We Exist," he wrote three statements:

1. *What we are most passionate about:*
2. *What we can do better than anyone else:*
3. *What drives our economic engine:*

"Why do I recognize these statements?" Rob asked.

"Because, my friend, you too have read **Good to Great**!" Sam replied. "These are the 'Hedgehog Concept' questions."

"Ah, yes, of course!"

"What the heck is a Hedgehog Concept?" Dave asked.

"It's based on a famous essay by Isaiah Berlin, a Russian-British social and political theorist and philosopher," Sam replied. "He described the battle between the fox and the hedgehog as an allegory for business competition. Foxes are quite clever, and they leverage a multitude of strategies to attack hedgehogs. Hedgehogs, however, possess a core knowledge of one big thing—how to morph into a sphere of protruding spikes and thus become impervious to attack from any direction. The hedgehog always wins despite the different tactics the fox uses. The good to great companies that Jim Collins and the ***Good to Great*** team studied had a deep understanding of a core principle that would always allow them to outmaneuver competitors and win."

"That's a weird name for such a brilliant concept," Dave said, standing. He grabbed a green marker and completed the three statements:

1. What we are most passionate about: ***Doing what's never been done.***
2. What we can do better than anyone else: ***Influence strategy and execute with excellence.***
3. What drives our economic engine: ***Driving sales of Goltur.***

"Yeah!" Sam exclaimed. "You're basically pulling from the values and motivators. I like where this is going!"

"I do too," Rob said, getting up to join his compatriots. He grabbed a red marker and approached the whiteboard to make some important edits:

1. What we are most passionate about: *Doing what's never been done.* **by revolutionizing the lives of appropriate patients with high cholesterol.**
2. What we can do better than anyone else: ~~*Influence strategy and execute with excellence.*~~ **Transform**

quality ideas into exceptional execution.

3. What drives our economic engine: ~~Driving sales of Goltur~~. **Making Goltur the brand of choice for appropriate patients with high cholesterol.**

Dave scrunched up his face as Rob marked up his work like a fifth grade grammar teacher, but even he had to admit that the edits were the right ones. "Damn, you're good," he said once Rob had finished.

"Okay!" Sam said, clearly energized. "Let's do the same for the next two columns. And let's pressure test this using the Rule of Proactivity from **The Seven Habits of Highly Effective People**."

Rob raised his eyebrow.

"We need to ensure that the answers are fully within our Circle of Control," Sam clarified.

* * *

They continued to work through the weekend on the three columns, commandeering Sam's dining room at home (to Patricia's chagrin), putting in three hours on Saturday and another three on Sunday. The final plan came together in a visual narrative called **Our Culture**.

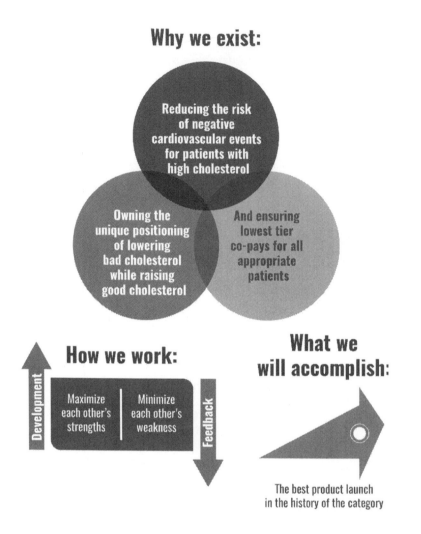

Why we exist:

Reducing the risk of negative cardiovascular events for patients with high cholesterol

Owning the unique positioning of lowering bad cholesterol while raising good cholesterol

And ensuring lowest tier co-pays for all appropriate patients

How we work:

Development

Maximize each other's strengths

Minimize each other's weakness

Feedback

What we will accomplish:

The best product launch in the history of the category

Every time he looked at the narrative, Sam got more excited, convinced that they were on the right track. Still, he needed a second opinion.

"Hi, Logan, I trust you received my email?"

"Yes, Sam. It's open in front of me right now."

"Excellent. So, what do you think?"

"Well, Sam," Logan replied. "I'm not going to tell you what I think. The only thing that matters is whether this culture road map will lead to results."

"Very true," Sam agreed. "I get it. You are coaching and not mentoring me at this point. I guess I just wanted to thank you for inspiring me with the basic training conversation."

"Anytime, Sam. That'll be five thousand dollars!" he said, laughing.

"Send the bill!" Sam replied. "I'll let you know how it goes, Logan. Take care."

The next step was to build awareness. Sam asked Gaile to create large posters that were to be hung in each colleague's office, *Declaration of Independence*-style. He dedicated a staff meeting to the *why*s, *how*s, and *what*s of their culture, and got buy-in from each team member. Each colleague was randomly quizzed by their bosses about the three questions. Those who answered correctly got to park in the executive lot for a week, and those who did not were given a cactus.

The cactus concept was Rob's idea. It was a prickly, ugly, thirsty reminder of failure. He intoned correctly that no one would want the cactus sitting on their desk for too long. It worked even better than Sam imagined, becoming the team's version of latrine duty.

Dave suggested that they socialize their ways of working beyond the core team—up and out. They mapped the key stakeholders and took them through the *why*s, *how*s, and *what*s of their team culture. Before long, Sam started seeing different cars rotating in the executive parking lot and a few cactuses.

But more important than that, they were starting to get things done and move at a much faster pace.

Who knew that culture could be so powerful?

CHAPTER EIGHT:

INFECTIOUS INFLUENCE

Norming – Six months to launch

It was bound to happen eventually, but the timing was terrible. Six months before the launch of Goltur, Sam's knee gave out while he was walking to the parking garage. Lying facedown on the cold concrete, he considered all the wear and tear the joint had seen over his forty-seven years on earth. Humans were mechanical creatures. Complex, sure, but not built to last.

Sam flew down to North Carolina to see his good friend, Dr. Drew Prince, one of the top orthopedic surgeons in the country.

"You want the bad news, or the bad news?" Dr. Drew asked him after the MRI results came back.

"There's no good news?"

"Of course there's good news," Dr. Drew replied. "There isn't a knee on God's green earth I haven't been able to repair thus far."

"Then why didn't you lead with that?!" Sam exclaimed.

"Because, Sam, I can't fix your knee. It's unsalvageable."

"Unsalvageable? What are you saying, Doc?"

"There is no surgical route to improve the situation."

"That certainly is bad news then. And you say there's

more bad news?"

"Yes. I've been experimenting with biomechanical knees and have the perfect model for you."

"Um, that sounds like good news."

"Wait for it," Dr. Drew replied. "It's true that I can fit you with a completely new knee. The bad news is that you will need at least eight weeks to recover."

Eight weeks! He'd be out of commission until ninety days before launch. He couldn't do it. Decision made, Sam tried to stand up, then remembered he was in a wheelchair.

"How soon can we schedule the procedure?" he asked.

The next morning, Gaile arranged a teleconference so he could deliver the news to his team. He would work from home for the next month before the procedure, and then for the following two months as well. He'd already prepped Jim, Rob, and Dave on what needed to happen in the intervening weeks and put them in charge of the next big deliverable— the final launch-readiness business review on June 30. Sam assured Jim and the rest of the team that he would be back on his feet by then.

* * *

Sam had never been out of the office for more than two weeks and working from home was killing him. Technology didn't help, with web and teleconference systems regularly acting up. The good news was that the team kept him cheery by starting a joke and riddle of the day

WhatsApp group. Sam was sure Patricia thought he was losing it—on more than one occasion she'd walked into his makeshift command center in the study and found him laughing uproariously to himself.

The other silver lining of working from home was that Sam was forced to focus on only the essential deliverables. Besides the final business review, Giant and Harris were currently in a major debate about whether to invest in direct-to-consumer advertising for Goltur upon launch. Harris's robust marketing process indicated that there was a fifty-fifty chance of success. Sam, Rob, and Jim, however, favored an aggressive strategy of achieving rapid insurance coverage for Goltur at the lowest co-pay tier for patients. If they could accomplish this by year's end, consumer advertising would be a masterful stroke. By educating patients on the power of raising "good" cholesterol while simultaneously lowering "bad" cholesterol—an idea called "Take the Good with the Bad," which was coined by their consumer advertising guru Hank Lowenstein—they could significantly boost the launch outlook.

Sam dedicated his time at home to meeting key players one-on-one so he could identify the barriers they presented to gaining agreement from Harris about the consumer-advertising plan. He soon learned that the largest of those barriers came in the form of Aaron Jameson, the Harris head of the joint venture. Harris had recently been burned by the failure of their pain reliever, Caldor, and were therefore in a highly risk-averse mindset. Sam's objective was to move Aaron across the line into the consumer-advertis-ing-positive camp. Sam's confidence that he had the right stuff to get it done was bolstered by the knowledge that he possessed three talents in the influencing domain from the Clifton Strengths® assessment.

Sam decided to intentionally use his Maximizer and Communication talents in tandem by inquiring into Aaron's concerns about consumer advertising and advocating a message of continuous improvement.

"I think I've been quite clear on my concerns with consumer advertising, Sam," Aaron responded to Sam's probe.

"Not as clear as we'd like, Aaron. We want to understand if the issue is cost or if the issue relates to a risk your models have identified."

"Fair enough. The issue is that the market research right now is very inconclusive about whether this message of good and bad cholesterol will play widely in all of our key demographics. Since we can't model the impact, we don't feel the 'spray and pray' approach is the way to go."

"We fully agree with you, Aaron. No one is advocating for wasting valuable resources. What we want is to move beyond market research and pilot the concept in a few key markets to see if it's got any legs. We'd collect the data necessary to fill in the blanks in your models, and if it appears to have potential, we could then scale up the investment level commensurate with the anticipated return. How does that sound?"

"A lot more reasonable, but you know I can't unilaterally approve such a plan."

"Of course not. How much time do you need?" Sam asked.

"Let me get back to you in a few days."

Sam's strategy eventually worked, and Harris begrudgingly agreed to fund exploratory consumer-advertising pilots in selected markets linked to favorable insurance access. Jim and Rob were very happy with this result, and Jim commented that Sam did his best work lying down!

With that off his plate, Sam turned his attention to his upcoming operation. He'd been researching everything he could about this new "bionic" knee they would be implanting into his body. While flying was going to be difficult after the procedure, overall, he should see a reduction in pain. The literature suggested that the relief could last up to twenty years. The procedure, known as a total knee replacement, was generally quite safe. The worst complications were blood clots and a very small chance of pulmonary embolism. Sam focused on the positive parts of the outcome and imagined himself back on the golf course soon.

The big day arrived. Sam was nervous but put on a brave face for his family. Despite having worked in healthcare for twenty years, he hated hospitals. Still, he loved doctors and knew he was in the hands of consummate professionals as well as a friend. The last thing he remembered before the anesthesia took hold was Dr. Drew leaning over him and quipping, "I wonder how much your kidneys will fetch on the black market…"

The procedure was a complete success. Sam acquired a brand-new titanium alloy mobile-bearing prosthetic knee courtesy of the fine folks at Zimmer Biomet. Within twenty-four hours post operation, he was standing and walking with the help of a walker and his new physical therapist—a Swedish woman named Monica Svenson. Her job would be to torture him for the next five days until he was discharged.

During this intense recovery process, Sam reflected on why he'd joined a pharmaceutical company right out of college so many years back. The healthcare industry got a bad rap. To the public, negative impressions were widespread: drugs were too expensive, hospitals bankrupted people, physician's drug-prescribing patterns were overtly influenced by greedy sales reps, the FDA was in bed with Monsanto, and it was all funded by evil pharmaceutical company CEOs. But people lost sight of one simple fact—this industry, while not perfect, did far more good than harm. They'd pretty much eradicated polio, for God's sake! Sam committed to remind himself and his team of this more often to keep them focused on why they came to work every day.

Sam was discharged from the hospital after four days and placed on a rigorous PT and diet regimen designed to accelerate his recovery. Because of his relatively young age and good overall health, Dr. Drew and Monica felt they could meet the timeline to get him back in the office before the final review with management on June 30. Sam focused on maximizing his circle of control by making the necessary daily commitment to his recovery and practiced regular bucket filling with his loved ones. With each passing week, the knee grew stronger and his attitude improved. He documented his journey back to full health in a journal—this story would serve as great motivation for the sales force at the launch, as it helped him capture the moments of pain, frustration, hope, fear, and focus.

Of course, he stayed in touch with the happenings at the office. Everything appeared to be going as planned—either that, or Rob and Dave weren't telling him the entire truth to help him focus on his rehabilitation. Sam wouldn't blame them if that were the case, and he was thankful. Not having to worry about work allowed him to concentrate on getting better.

Before long, six weeks had passed since the procedure. Gone was the swelling and inflammation, and he had a greatly improved range of motion in his knee. He'd been walking unassisted for the past month, and Monica had allowed him to begin doing some more intense exercise on the stationary bike. In his weekly video catch-up with Dr. Drew, he got some unexpected good news.

"Well, Sam, looks like you're well enough to return to the office. Just keep doing your daily PT and be sure to walk ten thousand steps every day. Don't stay seated all day or that knee may swell up again."

On Tuesday, May 27, seven weeks after undergoing a total knee replacement, Sam walked into the Giant headquarters and got back to work. For once, he arrived before eight o'clock. He found Dave in his office writing on a flip chart, his back to the door.

"What you got there, CC?" Sam asked.

Dave turned around, clearly surprised.

"Coach! Welcome back!" Dave walked over to give Sam a handshake and a hug. "How's the super knee? We've got a bet going as to whether you can dunk with that thing—please say you can, or I'm out fifty dollars!"

"I missed you guys, too, Dave," Sam replied. "But there will be no dunking of anything other than donuts."

"Ah, a great loophole! They didn't specify *slam* dunk," Dave replied, winking.

Sam only half heard. He was examining the flip chart. On top were the words **Leader Board**, and beneath was a grid:

Execution	Influence	Relationship	Strategy
Marcus*	Jim	Gaile*	Rob*
Rebecca*	Sam*	Vignesh	Lincoln*
Sarah	Scott	Larry	Karen
Nate	Dave*	Dan	Hank
Greg	Alicia*	Chuckie	Alexandra

Beneath the grid was a list of prioritized deliverables related to the upcoming business review:

Execution	Influence	Relationship	Strategy
Root-cause analysis for performance issues **Rebecca**	Cross-functional team agendas **Dave**	Stakeholder maps in key accounts **Larry**	Market research results **Lincoln**
Sales force effectiveness tracking **Sarah**	Brand review agenda and "Story" **Alicia**	Internal marketing campaign **Chuckie**	Consumer-advertising pilot results **Hank**
Weekly progress meeting **Marcus**	Sales force training agenda **Alicia**	Post brand review celebration planning **Gaile**	Pricing research results **Rob**
	Best practice collection and communication **Alicia/Karen**	Re-read walkthrough sessions with internal stakeholders **Vignesh**	Induet Inspires initiative ROI **Alexandra**
40	25	35	30

On the very bottom of the flip chart were points. The execution team appeared to be in the lead.

"Explain this to me," Sam said.

"Well, in our culture we maximize strengths and minimize weaknesses, right? After you left, we were still struggling with shared accountability, so I consulted with Missy, and she suggested we try gamifying our work. I asked our extended team to take the Clifton Strengths® assessment and then mapped everyone to the four strength domains. When we include the extended team, we have all four domains covered; without the extended team, we're thin in the Execution and Relationship-Building domains. Next, we needed to apply the talents to the projects we were working on. We decided to focus on just one—the business review. So, we broke down the deliverables and assigned them to the four teams. On a weekly basis, we are tracking progress against each deliverable and assigning points by domain. Every week there is a new winner, and they get to leave work at noon on Friday. The losing team gets the cactus! Make sense?"

Sam was dumbfounded. "Wow, Dave—I love it! You've figured out a way to harness the team's unique talents against our work objectives. And it seems to be working?"

"So far, so good. But our influence team is bringing up the rear—you've got some cactus watering to do!"

"How did each colleague get assigned to their respective domain?" Sam asked.

"Anyone with multiple talent themes in a domain was mapped to that area."

"And what about their other talents in the other domains?"

"Well, as you know, most people are concentrated in a few areas based on their top five signature themes. Missy says as we mature as a team, we should consider getting the full thirty-four-theme report for the whole team because themes one through ten are the most dominant areas. This would adjust for any missteps from looking at the top five alone."

"This is amazing, Dave, really," Sam replied. "How did you get everyone to buy in? Wasn't there some resistance and skepticism to overcome?"

"We did most of the legwork by getting everyone to adopt our culture. The **Leader Board** is just a natural extension of how we work. Once people had a working knowledge of their unique talents and had visibility into everyone else's, it just kind of came together. Of course, it hasn't been without speed bumps, but by and large, it seems to be working."

"I guess that makes sense," Sam said. "So, what do I need to get done this week? I want this cactus off my desk!"

CHAPTER NINE:
PRODUCTIVE CONFLICT

Norming – Three months to launch

"This pricing strategy will never work," said Richard di Fiore, Giant's new CFO. "Are you seriously advocating to price Goltur for less than we sell each of the components for today? Why should we just leave money on the table?"

The boardroom grew silent. Alexandra Lubantik, VP of Finance, was presenting this section of the Goltur launch-readiness business review, and Sam saw her face flush. *Go on, Alex*, he thought, *we prepared for this*. His mind returned to the day they'd first discussed the pricing issue as a team.

* * *

Shortly after his return to the office, Sam called for a top-to-bottom review of the presentation. It soon became apparent that there was conflict brewing between the four domain committees. Rob's strategic direction was to focus the presentation around the four Ps of their approach: product, price, place, and promotion. The Execution committee, chaired by Rebecca, found this flow to be unwieldy and overcomplicated. Relationship-Building was pushing for a hybrid version, while Alicia advocated for a completely different presentation structure altogether.

They convened in the Darwin Room to naturally select the fittest approach for the review. In attendance was his staff (Rob, Alicia, Lincoln, Marcus, Dave, and Rebecca), the Global Goltur/Induet team (Scott Denger, senior director of global marketing; Greg Bundy, director of global market access; and Vignesh Neeru, associate product manager), and their key support functions (Hank Lowenstein, VP of direct-to-consumer advertising; Karen Salinger, public relations; Sarah Richardson, director of analytics; Larry Streeter, director of managed care; Dan Sarver, director of marketing operations; Alexandra Lubantik, VP of finance; Nate Spinola, director of finance; and Luca Rizzo, senior VP of cardiovascular research and development). Sam was glad that Gaile was ordering sandwiches—gaining alignment would be tough with a group this size.

"Okay, team," Sam opened. "I'm aware of the diverging perspectives on the approach to the presentation. Alicia, I hear you've got some 'hot off the press' information for us."

"I sure do, Coach. We asked Gaile to get the scoop on the Benzyte launch review. She spoke to a few folks who were in the room who said the four Ps approach bombed!"

"It bombed because Greg Nielson is a wooden presenter," Lincoln countered. "We've got Coach, Rob, and Dave!"

"That wasn't the only reason it didn't go well," Larry chimed in. "The presentation collapsed in the pricing section. Richard eviscerated them on their assumptions. It was brutal."

"Our pricing story is airtight," Marcus countered. "Richard will be eating out of Alexandra's hands."

Alexandra didn't seem convinced. "This is not a lay-up, guys," she said. "Remember that there's a joint venture board meeting with Harris a few days before our presentation. We aren't exactly singing from the same sheet music yet on pricing."

"Can we table this conversation?" Scott asked. "How are we going to tee up the Germany issue?"

Germany issue? This was news to Sam. He'd have to follow up with Scott about that later. Right now, they needed to move this conversation toward some sort of resolution. He looked over at Dave to intervene, but Dave didn't seem at all perturbed by the discussion.

"The evidence points to the 4 Ps being fraught with more risk than product, market, and execution," Alicia interjected. "May I present the flow so everyone can throw rocks at it?"

"Works for me," Rob replied, pulling the conversation back on topic. "We should look at both. That way we can compare and contrast."

Heads nodded around the conference room at this suggestion. Sam was thankful Jim wasn't here to witness this debacle. What was happening to his team? He'd often thought of them as a football squad where he called the plays and his group executed the plan. Now it seemed like everyone was trying to call the shots despite the clear accountabilities mapped on the **Leader Board**. The lack of team unity and vision bothered him.

After both Alicia and Lincoln presented their respective approaches to the presentation, it was clear that an *and* approach was needed. By taking Lincoln's superior product section and marrying it with Alicia's brilliant execution section, they had a flow everyone could agree with. The Goltur pricing strategy was also much more clearly linked with how to maximize managed care access. Although pleased with the outcome, Sam still had concerns about the process they'd taken to get there. He told Dave as much over beers that evening.

Dave countered with a simple question: "How would you have arrived at the same outcome without that debate?"

Sam thought about it. "I don't know. But I didn't like the tension between everyone," he complained. "Seemed counterproductive."

"I can see your point, Coach," Dave replied between sips of beer. "But let me tell you what I saw. I saw passion. I saw our second line learning how to defend a perspective. And then I saw everyone come together, align on a path forward, and agree on next steps and accountabilities. I saw trust between team members and confidence that we could arrive at the right decision together. Have you read *The Five Dysfunctions of a Team* by Patrick Lencioni?"

"It's on my list, but I haven't gotten to it yet."

"In the book, Lencioni tells a leadership fable about a leader in Silicon Valley who inherits a dysfunctional leadership team and, using specific tactics, transforms them into a high-performing unit. Lencioni lays out a pyramid of team cohesiveness that starts with absence of trust on the lowest level and ends with inattention to results on the highest level."

Dave grabbed a napkin and took a few moments to draw a simple diagram:

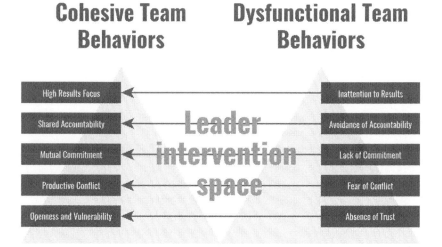

Cohesive Team Behaviors

Dysfunctional Team Behaviors

Cohesive Team Behaviors		Dysfunctional Team Behaviors
High Results Focus	← Leader	Inattention to Results
Shared Accountability	← intervention	Avoidance of Accountability
Mutual Commitment	← space	Lack of Commitment
Productive Conflict	←	Fear of Conflict
Openness and Vulnerability	←	Absence of Trust

"Lencioni describes five stages of dysfunction and the corresponding opposites that are needed to build cohesiveness," Dave said, referencing the diagram. "It's the leader's responsibility to move a team from the dysfunctional side to the cohesive side."

Sam studied the diagram. "I need more time to digest the model, but it seems relatively intuitive. Are you saying that our team has a 'fear of conflict'?"

"Not anymore, as you saw from the meeting!" Dave chuckled. "After you went on leave, everyone was being too damn polite, and you know I don't have the patience for that type of nonsense. So, I started encouraging debates in our staff meetings. Soon enough, people started opening up. The trust was already there, so it just took a little push. Once we started debating, we got more inputs, and the more the team felt heard, the easier it was to mutually decide on where we wanted to go. We have a very responsible group, so shared accountability was pretty easy from there. But it all started from productive conflicts."

Sam gave Dave a hearty pat on the back. "I stand corrected, Dave. I guess this type of conflict can be quite instructive and constructive!"

"We're just building off the progress made in the offsite meeting," Dave said. "Put people in their strength zones and then empower them to deliver. That's the idea, right?"

* * *

Now in the boardroom, Sam saw an opportunity for productive conflict on a higher level.

"It's a fair challenge, Richard," he said, stepping in before Alexandra could answer. "We've had extensive debate on this issue and have concluded that with the current price pressures in the healthcare environment, the strategic play would be to take the issue off the table for insurers and not force them to choose between covering Induet *or* covering Goltur. We want to help them make the *and* choice, and this pricing proposal is one way to achieve that. Of course, we welcome your inputs."

Sam could feel his team's bulging eyes boring into him from all sides. This was not what they'd rehearsed. Still, he was heeding the lesson Dave had taught him: sometimes the process wasn't pretty, but if the desired result was achieved and everyone had a chance to have their say, the conflict was worth it.

Richard cleared his throat to respond, but Myra beat him to it. "It's bold, Sam. But I'm not sure Harris will buy it. We saw very different pricing at the board meeting a few days back."

"They'll buy it, Myra," Jim interjected. "Their own models show slower volume uptake at anything above a five-to-eight-percent premium over Induet's current average wholesale price. All we have to do is get them to run the same model with these numbers. And that's our ask of you. Take this proposal over and insist on seeing the data before approving the pricing. Our rudimentary models show a volume increase of around twenty-five percent in year one, which more than offsets any benefit we would see from a higher entry price."

"I wouldn't classify our models as rudimentary, Jim," Richard said, finally getting his chance to chime in. "Alexandra, take me through the numbers. Once I'm satisfied, I'll call Harris."

Alex—whose number one talent theme was Analytical—had the data at the ready on a thumb drive and proceeded to review the numbers in front of the senior executives. Due to the impromptu debate, they eventually aligned on a price that was slightly higher than Sam's original proposal but significantly lower than Harris's recommendation. At Myra's insistence, Harris confirmed the expected sales bump with their own models, and once the data was out in the open, it became obvious to the joint venture board which course of action to take.

* * *

As the countdown to launch sped toward its inevitable conclusion, Sam continued to reap the benefits of the productive
conflict approach. In their cross-functional meetings, he started
to hear from people who usually played the background. One
of his biggest worries about encouraging debate was that
while his more strategic- and influence-minded team members
battled it out, his relationship builders would be turned off
and executors grow bored as they waited for clarity. And there
was some of that, but Dave was an expert at orchestrating and
mediating these debates. Strategic thinkers always wanted to
weigh in on the *how*, whereas influencers focused on understanding the *why*, executors the *what*, and relationship builders
on *who*. Dave simply introduced dialogues that allowed for
all these viewpoints to be present.

Meetings were lively and spirited. All viewpoints were
included, and Sam noticed that the quality of the decisions
and outcomes they took as a team markedly improved. He
went from skeptic to ardent supporter in record time. This
was timely, because the biggest challenges were right around
the corner.

The Goltur launch was imminent!

CHAPTER TEN:

KNOW AND OWN YOUR ROLE

Performing – Launch!

Sam prepared to test both his team's effectiveness and the strength of his new knee as he boarded the corporate jet to fly to Chicago for the biggest launch of his career. To think, fourteen months earlier he'd been concerned about losing his job! The fear was still there, but if he did get canned, it would be due to the ineffectiveness of his leadership. Sam pushed the negativity aside and focused his attention on the week to come. Failure was not an option.

Before he left the office, Gaile had provided him with the "book"—a binder that contained, day by day, every detail of the event, clearly demarcated and laid out. They'd conducted a train-the-trainer session two weeks prior to ensure that the district managers (DMs) could lead their teams through the launch sessions, and Sam realized just how many new district managers they'd onboarded for the launch. Gaile had prepared a one-page bio for each DM, and he planned to use the two-hour flight to memorize as many of the ninety-two names as possible.

Sam realized that if his biggest concern while flying next to Jim, Myra, and Chief Operating Officer Luke Stockley was remembering nearly a hundred names, things were very well in hand. This launch was such a big deal for Harris and Giant that presentations would be given by both CEOs, both research & development heads, both presidents, both heads of sales, and the joint venture head—leaving a very small slot of airtime for Sam and his Harris marketing counterpart. Although he loved the stage and the bright lights, he was happy to cede the responsibility of motivating the troops to the heavy hitters.

Speaking of motivating the troops, at the train-the-trainer meeting, Alicia had the brilliant idea to put the DMs through the exact same training that their sales reps would be going through at the launch meeting. This would ensure comprehensive understanding of the training and alignment with the approach. At first, Sam had been skeptical, but the data Dave and Alicia presented after the final day of the train-the-trainer was impressive. The DMs were ready.

"Ninety-eight percent of the DMs agree or strongly agree that they are ready to lead the breakout sessions based on the train-the-trainer," Alicia had said. "And this is a representative sample of nearly ninety-five percent of the district managers."

"Where did you get this data?" Sam asked.

"One of the benefits of investing in INTERACT," Dave replied. "The app lets us poll the audience, receive questions in real time, send field surveys, and conduct quizzes and learning games all from the iPad. The data is generated and analyzed on the spot. INTERACT allows us to gauge participant understanding and alignment, reinforce our key messages, and answer many more questions—in real time."

Sam was very glad Dave had convinced him to use this new system not only for the train-the-trainer, but for the launch as well. INTERACT would ensure they'd have a finger on the pulse of the entire sales force while keeping the engagement level high. He flipped to the first page of the "book," which described the objectives for the week of meetings ahead:

- Build belief (science, product profile)
- Increase knowledge (disease, mechanism of action, competitive landscape, product positioning, key messages)
- Apply skills (message delivery model, transitioning between products, closing)
- Finalize planning (top thirty-five customers routing, resource allocation, launch programs)

Their mission was clear. But there was still a ton that could go wrong and a very small margin for error. Everyone would have to give their best effort and sustain that through the week. It was going to take the collective culture he'd been building from the outset to pull it all off.

They were going to have to keep negativity and worries at bay by focusing on what they could control when inevitable problems arose. They would have to demonstrate exceptional individual and collective work ethic, heart, optimism, and maturity. They would need to be servant leaders and ensure that the sales force felt truly supported and prepared to overcome the challenges waiting for them in the market. They would have to harness all their actions behind the single intent of delivering a world-class launch from the ground up. Sam would need to count on each colleague's individual and unique talents, strengths, and collective domains and put them in position to shine. Their culture would be on display for all to see this week. The **Leader Board** would be in full effect, and they would need to trust productive conflict to bring out the best solutions as necessary.

In short, it was time for each colleague to know and own their role.

Sam flipped to the second page of the "book"—the division of responsibility and leader board for the launch.

Execution	Influence	Relationship	Strategy
Vendor orchestration **Marcus**	JV alignment **Dave**	Team dinners **Gaile**	Lead brand sessions with JV **Rob/Lincoln**
Role play certification **Rebecca**	PR liaison **Sam**	Recognition programs **Gaile**	Clarify strategy during breakout walkarounds **Lincoln**
Daily summaries and comms **Rebecca**	Endomarketing and social media **Alicia**	VIP herding **Gaile**	
Training collateral **Rebecca**			
IT liaison **Marcus**			
War room schedule **Marcus**			

This would be the first "live fire" test of their team's DNA. Whatever happened during the week would define how the team functioned moving forward.

* * *

"This is not even close to being ready," Marcus confessed to Rebecca. "Where the heck are the leaders' guides? We shipped them over a week ago, and there's nothing here!" He gestured wildly at the near-empty Fed-Ex/UPS office where they were standing.

"Take a deep breath, Marcus," Rebecca replied. "You're going to hyperventilate."

"Okay, okay," Marcus said, trying to calm down.

"That's better. Allowing negativity to fester isn't going to get us anywhere. We need to focus on what we can control in this situation—and what we currently control is what phone calls we make to get the conference center shipping department on the case."

"I hear you, but Coach is gonna flip if we can't find these leaders' guides before he gets here for our walk-through!"

"Well, we've got about ninety minutes to avoid that scenario," she replied, showing Marcus the text on her phone. "The eagle has landed!"

* * *

Rob walked into the INTERACT command center to see how Lincoln was progressing with the final tweaks to the meeting application. The small, poorly lit conference room was crammed with people and peripherals. Lincoln sat at a round table near the door, and the rest of the INTERACT team was huddled around a server in the back. Dozens of iPads were stacked on the table, a tangle of cords in the center. Rob surveyed the scene—this place looked more like an Apple graveyard than a command center.

"Hey Rob," Lincoln said, looking up. "You look nice and fresh."

"And you don't!" Rob scolded. "You've got saddlebags under your eyes, mate, and I'm wondering which number Red Bull you're on at this point." He pointed to three empty energy drink canisters.

"No time for sleep, Rob. Not until I confirm that the polling is working one hundred percent. This morning it was only loading sixty-five percent of the time!"

"Understood, Lincoln. And I admire your dedication but let me take over for a bit. Go next door, take a one-hour nap, shower, shave, and be back here in time for the walk-through."

Lincoln eventually relented and left Rob in charge. Rob approached the INTERACT team and said, "Okay boys and girls—what's our contingency plan if we can't get this polling running?"

* * *

Dave stared at the rows and rows of chairs stretching out before him, amazed at the size of the room. It looked more like an airplane hangar than a meeting space, and in less than twelve hours it would be packed to capacity with six thousand staff from the collective Harris and Giant sales forces.

Dave reviewed the opening session agenda and speaking order for the umpteenth time. "This is the final order?" Dave asked Alicia.

"The last three versions I approved were supposed to be 'final,' but that hasn't stopped anyone from making yet another change to the schedule," she stated, a tinge of annoyance in her voice. "Instead of playing politics, we need to focus on what really matters—how this session will contribute to building sales force belief in Goltur."

"I hear you, Striker, and I share your frustration. How do you want to handle these continued changes?"

"Well, people really only remember the first and last thing they hear, right? I say we focus on bolstering Sam's finale, and let them rearrange the middle order as much as they want."

"That's good, Alicia! And I know exactly how to convince the joint venture marketing head to take a diminished role in that last segment."

Alicia looked incredulous. "How?"

"I'm going to tell her that Sam is adamant that he opens the segment and she closes."

"She'll think the opening is the better slot and will insist Sam closes. Brilliant!"

"The force is strong with this one," Dave said with a wink.

* * *

Gaile felt her blazer pocket vibrate for the fifth time as she made yet another trip between the hotel and the convention center. Realizing that something must be going on, she stopped and accessed the screen. Two missed calls from Rebecca, a text from Rob, a text from Dave, and a text from Sam. She dialed voice mail while reading the three text messages:

From Sam: Is Myra's conference room ready to go? She has a call as soon as we get in.

From Rob: Please make sure Lincoln actually goes to sleep!

From Dave: Can you locate the JV marketing head for me?

The calls were from Rebecca. "Hi Gaile, it's Rebecca. Do you have a manager-level contact at the convention center for shipping?"

Rebecca again. "Never mind on the manager; we just corralled him. Can you give Marcus a call and use your mystical soothing powers to let him know everything is going to work out?"

And to think that Gaile had wondered if she'd be useful at such a big meeting! She responded to each message and called Marcus before resuming her preparation for the evening's social gathering. The party had to be perfect—she had a feeling the team was going to have a lot to celebrate.

* * *

Sam sat in the front row of the packed auditorium next to the top executives of Giant and Harris, waiting for the announcer to introduce him to the stage. Although as big as an airplane hangar, the room was warm with the kinetic energy of excitement and shared purpose. After his brief closing remarks, the dog and pony portion of the meeting would conclude, with the rest of the week dedicated to the task of transforming the motivation and positive energy from the plenary sessions into the clarity of purpose, strength of capability, and power of coordination necessary to deliver a best-in-class launch. The idea he wanted to get across in his talk was relatively simple but would require exquisite execution to connect the dots between their collective *why* and give these six thousand strong medical representatives a vision of what it would take to win.

While drafting his comments, Sam had reflected on all the many stumbles and falls (some literal) he'd endured over the course of his career that had led him to this incredible moment. He thought about the extreme gratitude he had for the process and the learning, endurance, and resilience he'd gained during his journey. He would endeavor to share a bit of his personal perspective to prepare this massive and extremely diverse group for the challenges that lay ahead. And he wanted them to believe that despite all odds, they would find a way to succeed, together.

The talk centered on three concepts he'd actively applied on the journey to this moment—**W.H.O.M.**, **INNERviews**, and the **Leader Board**. To win, they had to outwork their competition, demonstrate their shared passion for patients each day, apply effective solution orientation, and exercise high maturity to overcome the inevitable disagreements and disappointments that would occur. To succeed, Giant and Harris would need to go beyond superficial relationships and really get to know each other's strengths on a deeper level to extract true value from the synergy of the two enterprises in this shared quest. To win, they would need their collective leaders in Strategic Thinking, Relationship Building, Influencing, and Execution to work in productive harmony so they could innovate and iterate constantly, fail faster, adapt more quickly, and overdeliver on their shared objectives.

The announcer interrupted Sam's thoughts, saying, "And now to close off today's plenary session, Sam Lombardi, senior director of marketing, Giant Pharmaceuticals."

Sam stood up on his new "bionic" knee and walked slowly and confidently to the stage. He'd elected to forego a teleprompter and just speak from his prepared notes. The lights were too bright to see too far into the crowd, so Sam imagined his merry band of misfits, his board of leaders, looking up at him and willing him the positive energy to knock one out of the park. He gave a broad smile to the audience and clicked to his first image.

"This is a picture of my mom, Claire. Three years ago, Harris Pharmaceuticals helped save her life after she had a heart attack and was prescribed Lotor to keep her bad cholesterol levels down. A little over a year later, Giant Pharmaceuticals further enriched my mom's life by providing even greater coronary artery protection by raising her good cholesterol with Induet. The combination of the science from these two incredible companies is already reducing the worries of people like me with dear relatives at risk of death or stroke due to their hereditary and lifestyle factors. And this week, this combination comes full circle with the launch of Goltur…"

* * *

The rest of the week passed in a blink for Sam and team. Every moment was filled with activity, and the group shared a singular focus—execute the plan. When Thursday night finally arrived, they were thankful for it. After months of planning and prep, they were ready to see Goltur take off.

The week of meetings had been a success and went off without a hitch. Now, sitting around a long banquet table inside the fine dining institution Spiaggia Chicago, it was time for some laughs and much-needed stress relief.

Comedy Central (aka Dave Maxwell) was up to the challenge, cracking jokes from start to finish. Sam transformed key moments from the week into new legends that would be spun by each team member for years to follow. During an emotional toast, Rob provided thoughtful commentary and insights into the key role that everyone on the team had fulfilled. Alicia exuded new confidence and pure enthusiasm as she recanted how valuable the insights she gathered via the INTERACT platform had been. Lincoln crystallized his excitement about the impact they were about to make in the lives of millions of patients in the US and around the world. Marcus waxed poetic about the amazing work of the managed markets team, who had already secured significant access for the product across the country. Rebecca let them in on the exuberant comments she had gathered from her old colleagues in the field. And Gaile spoke of how proud she was to be part of such a unified and cohesive work family.

Just as Gaile wrapped up her thoughts, Jim Kelly arrived, having been invited to a celebratory meal between the Harris and Giant leadership teams down the street. He grabbed the empty seat left for him at the head of the table and took a moment to look at each person on the team.

"Well, well, well," he said after a moment. "Is this not the finest damn marketing team in the industry?"

"Hear, hear!" Sam echoed with the enthusiasm only great red wine and excellent company can provide.

"You guys really pulled it off," Jim continued. "Sam, you were given an extremely difficult task, and you have really exceeded expectations. Myra and our entire senior leadership team are truly appreciative of the enormous effort put forth by every one of you to make this launch meeting a sterling success. To commemorate the moment, I have two tokens of appreciation for each of you."

He nodded at the maître d', who instantly produced a shopping bag full of books. Jim passed the title around the table—John C. Maxwell's *The 17 Essential Qualities of a Team Player*. The book detailed several key attributes of great teammates.

"I bought this book," he said, "as a reminder that being a great team is a choice, not a given. When we get back home, the real work begins. We are going to be tested. Things are not going to go as planned. There will be failure. But in the end, if we adhere to the advice in this book, we will ultimately triumph!"

"Thanks a lot, Jim," Dave replied on behalf of the team. "We will definitely take this to heart, trust me. And I've read this one—it's awesome. But what's this you say about *another* token of appreciation?"

"Well," Jim replied with a coy smile. "Myra was so impressed with this launch that she's sending the corporate jet back tomorrow morning to ensure that her A team makes it back home in fitting style!"

Sam was blown away by the gesture. What a difference fourteen months made! Beaming, he studied his team, his heart swelling with pride. Tomorrow morning, they would be on top of the world—literally—if only for the ninety-five-minute flight from Chicago back to New Jersey. He was overwhelmed with gratitude—for his family, who'd been the bedrock of every success he'd ever enjoyed; for this wonderful group, who'd come together to deliver a fantastic product launch; for his boss for trusting and empowering him with such a crucial mission; and for his company for creating the opportunity in the first place by entering the deal with Harris. In this moment, all the hard work, uncertainty, worries, and stress evaporated, leaving a euphoria known only to those who accomplish much through the power of team.

FOUR WEEKS LATER

Performing?

The euphoria didn't last. It was Monday morning, four weeks post launch, and what Sam was seeing in the latest launch key performance indicator (KPI) dashboard was anything but stellar news. They'd missed the first month's sales target by 11 percent, and Jim was on the warpath. Everyone was pointing fingers at one another—Harris was saying that Giant wasn't securing product access fast enough, Giant was saying that Harris's sales team wasn't keeping up with executional KPIs, and nothing was getting resolved.

Sam called an emergency meeting so his crew and extended team could discuss how to address the issue. He looked around the room and saw a harrowed group at their collective wit's end. Folks had even begun to snipe at each other due to the stress of underachievement. As team leader, Sam needed to nip it all in the bud.

"Good morning, all," he started. "I don't need to beat a dead horse on this one—you've all seen the numbers. But as Myra always says, when the strategy is right, execution *is* the strategy. We know the strategy is right—all the indicators are still holding. Which means we need to identify the problems in our execution. But before we get to that, I want to address the executional issues I'm seeing amongst ourselves. Pressure can either burst pipes or make diamonds—it's up to us in terms of how we respond. Now, with that said, let's get down to business…"

DISCUSSION

Team Performance Acceleration Principles (TPAPs)

Forming	Storming	Norming	Performing*
1. Hire the right W.H.O.M.	6. Raise Your Leadership Lid	11. Enhance Team Trust	16. Foster Great Teamwork
2. Control over Concern	7. Team DNA	12. Encourage Productive Conflict	17. Inspect Expectations
3. Serve and Support	8. Get The INNERview	13. Enforce Commitments	18. Reward And Recognize
4. Fill buckets daily	9. WHY Before WHAT	14. Exercise Shared Accountability	19. Continuous Improvement Mindset
5. Keep Social Contracts	10. Connect The Dots	15. Execute Until Achievement	20. Stretch The Goalposts

*covered in Halo: The Mission of High-Performance Teams

SECTION I:

FORMING

Forming
1. Hire the right W.H.O.M.
2. Control over Concern
3. Serve and Support
4. Fill buckets daily
5. Keep Social Contracts

Executive Summary: Forming

Put yourself for a moment into the shoes of a sixteen-year-old kid on the first day of basketball practice after making the team. You are standing around in the gym with eleven other adolescents of roughly the same age, sizing up your peers. Some are taller than you, others are more athletic, a few are outwardly nervous, and several are stoic. People are gossiping about last year's team and how tough the coach is.

Suddenly, your coach appears and contemplates your group before saying, "Alright gang, let's get to work."

This example aptly describes the conditions at the beginning of the formation stage of a team. As a leader, you've got people of different capability, experience, and confidence levels, and it is up to you to make the most of this collective talent in service of your overarching goals. To do this, you must remain cognizant of the internal (e.g., thoughts and feelings) and external (e.g., behaviors and actions) worlds of your team members. Your responsibility is to harmonize these two states as soon as possible.

In the forming stage, your team is likely experiencing some of the following:

- Excitement
- Eagerness
- Anxiety
- Uncertainty

These thoughts and feelings may manifest themselves in the following behaviors and actions:

- Questioning everything
- Ignoring processes
- Testing your tolerance
- Disagreeing on team aims

Conventional guidance states that in this stage you should focus solely on directing the team and establishing clear objectives for both team and individual performance. Unfortunately, directing alone doesn't go far enough in ensuring that the team has reached the proper level of cohesion at the end of this stage.

Going back to the basketball team example, the coach explains to the team that your goal is to win the state championship and clarifies the role he sees for each member of the team. The starters and the bench players begin to separate into a natural hierarchy of talent, leaving some team members feeling demoralized. You do what the coach says out of respect for his or her title and experience, but not necessarily out of respect for him or her. Privately, the starters complain that the coach is crazy for believing a team with this level of talent can compete for a championship.

The **Leader Board** model for team formation starts with how you construct each piece. The guidance in this book recommends hiring people based on the Team Performance Acceleration Principle (TPAP) of **W.H.O.M.**—or **W**ork Ethic,

Heart, **O**ptimism, and **M**aturity (TPAP #1). This is accomplished by slowing down the hiring process to ensure you get the right building blocks from the start. It is highly recommended to have prospective team members audition for a role on the team by presenting a business case or performing some positionally relevant task to diminish biases on the part of the evaluators. If you are inheriting a team that you did not build yourself, then the first step is to assess the degree to which you have the right **W.H.O.M.** in place by taking the time to really get to know everyone on your team.

Once you hire those with the right **W.H.O.M.**, you need to demonstrate *how* you lead the team. The key principle here is focusing on what you can control versus focusing on concerns you cannot act upon (TPAP #2). You can address the team's excitement, anxiety, and uncertainty head on by conducting an exercise using Covey's three circles: Concern, Influence, and Control. In the early days of team formation, it is imperative to focus the team's actions on items within the circle of control and influence. This concentrated effort will result in quick wins for individuals and the team.

As the team begins acting on controllable and influenceable aspects of their work lives, roll up your sleeves and get to work right alongside them. Ensure that the goal is visible to all team members and everyone's role is clearly outlined, including your own as leader. Let the team know you exist to support their success by understanding their challenges and effectively serving them (TPAP #3) so they can focus on driving the business customer. Live the inverted triangle by diagnosing the root causes behind early errors, confusion, or misalignments, and support both individuals and the team to overcome these obstacles.

One great tool to leverage in the position of servant leader is daily bucket filling (TPAP #4). Leverage the power of positive impact tools such as smiles, support, courtesy, praise, care, recognition, laughter, listening, and observation, *especially* in the early days of team formation. This relaxes everyone, builds confidence, and encourages others to do the same, which creates a winning environment that will accelerate team cohesion. People perform best in supportive (yet challenging) environments where risk taking is encouraged, mistakes are forgiven, and success is regularly acknowledged. The more you fill the buckets of others, the more yours is filled in return, giving you a reservoir of positivity to dip into.

When you start to see successes accumulate across the team, or when a major milestone or deliverable is completed, unleash the power of social contracting (TPAP #5). Teams must work exceptionally hard in the early days to achieve success because talents are not readily known and/or appreciated, processes are not fully understood, and learning curves must be conquered. When you notice things starting to come together, take the team out for some informal bonding. Bonding *after* success allows people to celebrate in a relaxed setting, encouraging them to get to know each other better on a personal level. This will inspire the group to work together to achieve the next team goal even faster.

TPAP #1 – Hire the Right W.H.O.M.

This principle comes to life in Chapter Three of the story as Sam is building out his new team. A strong believer in the recommendations from *Good to Great* by Jim Collins and the principle of "First Who, Then What," Sam has identified work ethic, heart, optimism, and maturity—more than IQ or pedigree—as the attributes he prizes in team members. He also talks about the need to slow down the recruitment process to avoid hiring mistakes. We see him apply his **W.H.O.M.** process in the interview of Lincoln Stephens, who exceeds expectations in the conversation due to his transparency and vulnerability.

The link between team formation and hiring is quite explicit. As a leader, you need to know what you want and need in your people *before* you decide what is achievable. When the *what* comes before the whom, you may find yourself with a strong disconnect between the goals and the talent. Objectives are achieved *because* of the people involved, not despite them.

Key takeaways:
1. *Resume's lie*: As a document designed to put the candidate in their most flattering light, it is important not to overweight a candidate's self-evaluation. Prospective employees should be put through the paces: screenings,

culture fits, business cases, and dialogue with the hiring manager's boss. The various evaluators should then get together and compare notes on the candidate before aligning on a hiring decision.

2. *IQ and pedigree are not enough*: Intelligence and attendance at prestigious universities become less important when forming a team. A group of super-smart people may devolve into a battle for intellectual superiority, which won't help the work get done. Dig deeper than education to understand a candidate's dedication, drive, and resilience—attributes that will take a team much further.

3. *Back up your instincts*: Great interviewers are usually very instinctual. They judge a candidate less on what they say, and more on how they say it. Still, to avoid a bad hire, ensure you cast a wide net and use objective and subjective measures to assess a candidate's fit for your team.

4. *Define your W.H.O.M.*: What attributes do you value beyond intelligence and background? Design an assessment process that will allow a candidate to demonstrate these attributes, and stick to your guns. Set a minimum threshold and don't hire anyone who fails to meet your standards.

Applying this TPAP:

Break down your hiring process into sequential steps: Screening, culture fit, business case, and **W.H.O.M.** assessment. At every stage, a panel should convene to discuss the performance of candidates and reach consensus on who to advance, and why.

- Before posting an open position, create a great job description. According to Glassdoor.com, an effective job description performs the following functions (https://bit.ly/2VpEXbC):
    ○ Makes candidates aware of your open jobs and your organization.
    ○ Targets candidates right for the role to avoid the headache and time-consuming process of wading through unqualified resumes.
    ○ Maximizes your recruiting budget by attracting ideal-fit candidates and dissuading the less qualified from applying.
    ○ Avoids "Buyer's Remorse" from hires who regret coming on board, based on what they thought they knew about your company.

- Leverage behavior-based interviewing to screen for application of skills, knowledge, and experience. While this task is often driven by HR, it is fundamental that you, as the hiring manager, set the minimum bar for applicants to proceed to the next round. Behavior-based interviewing aims to predict future performance based on past situational behavior. (For a comprehensive list of behavioral screening questions, visit https://bit.ly/2Vt7HAj).

- Assess culture fit. Just because a candidate has the requisite knowledge, skills, and experience for a given job does not mean that they will fit into your company culture. By separating cultural fit from the behavioral screening process, you signal to both the applicant and your organization that fit is as important as ability. To maximize this step, you need to intrinsically understand and clearly articulate the cultural values that matter to your company and your team. If your company culture is relaxed, ask questions to assess what the candidate does to relax and de-stress. If your culture is competitive, ask questions to assess how the candidate feels about winning. Align each criterion with a different assessor and have candidates progress through each individual evaluator (ten-fifteen minutes each) focused on one aspect of culture fit. (For more basics related to effective values fit assessments, visit https://www.entrepreneur.com/article/250264).

- Candidates with the right behaviors and cultural values should then demonstrate their ability through a practical business case presentation. The value of a good business case is that it allows you to peek inside the candidate's brain and assess their ability to analyze information, prioritize, influence, and execute a plan. (For a business

case template from Harvard University, visit https://bit.
ly/2K92k8a).

- Once a candidate has successfully advanced through the
  preceding stages, there should be a final check by the
  hiring manager's manager. This is where the **W.H.O.M.**
  questions introduced in Chapter Three can be helpful.
  After this process has been completed, you can confidently state that a potential hire has the necessary skills,
  knowledge, and role experience; fits in with the company
  culture; can demonstrate their capability effectively in a
  business case setting; and has the requisite work ethic,
  shared passion, and solution orientation every team needs
  to succeed. (You can download the questionnaire below
  here: https://bit.ly/2D0P5ka).

Work Ethic	Heart	Optimism	Maturity
How do you judge a successful day?	What are your reasons for doing your best every day?	Describe the most stressful work situation you have encountered and how you handled it.	Describe a situation where you had an argument with a co-worker
How do your teammates rate you in terms of getting things done?	What are some of your hobbies and interests outside of work?	Tell me about a time when your superior came to you with a problem they wanted you to fix but you didn't knowhow, or waht to do.	Describe a situation whereyou were right but still had to follow instructions.
Tell me about a time when you overcame a significant challenge to finish a project on schedule.	What's one thing you're really proud of and why?	What are the biggest failures of your career so far?	Talk about a time when one of your ideas was challenged by colleague. What happened?
Describe a situation when you had to work as a member of a team to complete a task.	If we were to hire you, what do you seeing yourself doing here in three years?	Why do you think you willbe successful in this position?	Tell me about the most difficult decision you had to make recently.
Tell me about a time your workday ended before you were able to finish your tasks.	How have you helped others outside of work?	Give me an example where you helped a teammate achieve a goal where there was nothing in it for you.	How do you calm yourself down when you feel anxious or upset?
How do you remind yourself to complete projects and tasks?	Give me an example of something that you have focus on that took great courage and hard work to overcome.	Discuss a problem in your current role which you have yet to solve.	Tell me about a recent time a colleague disappointed you yet you still had to work together to complete a task.
When you have a lot of work to do, how do you get it all done? Give an example.	What excites you most about this opportunity?	Describe a situation where you had to collaborate with a difficult colleague.	Describe to me your biggest weakness and biggest strength.
Describe a situation when personal issues pulled you away from work and how you handled it?	What's the most fun you've ever had at work?	What do you do to de-stress?	Tell me about a colleague you really got along with and why you think you did.

- Ensure an effective onboarding process. While ***Leader-Board*** does not explicitly cover how to best onboard new team members, that does not mean it is not an essential step in the team-forming stage. The best companies (and leaders) design onboarding from the point of view of the employee, not the organization. ***The Best Place to Work*** by Ron Friedman states that when onboarding is done well, it helps new hires demonstrate competence and connect with other colleagues.

- Assign a first friend. Navigating a new company and team takes time. You can accelerate this by assigning a sociable member of your team to show the newcomer around, facilitate introductions, and explain how things work.

- Optimize the first ninety days. The initial journey into a new job is filled with questions. Encourage new joiners to lay out their key queries and map out a plan to ensure 90 percent of their questions get a satisfactory answer within three months. Here is a short template you can pass on to your onboarding colleagues: https://bit.ly/2YTMd1K

Discussing this TPAP:
1. How would you rate your current recruitment, selection, hiring, and onboarding process?
2. How much time do you personally invest in the recruitment, selection, hiring, and onboarding process? To what degree do you think your personal time investment is sufficient to ensure you hire candidates with the qualities you most value?
3. What are the attributes you value most in your

teammates and staff? Why?

4. To what degree is your team currently made up of these most desirable attributes? If the answer is below your expectation, what adjustments do you need to make to ensure the right behavioral expectations are reinforced and aligned?

5. What, if anything, do you need to adjust in your onboarding process to ensure new joiners gain clarity and confidence in their roles faster?

TPAP #2 – Control over Concern

In Chapter Two, we move into Sam's home life and see the congruence between his public and private personas. Sam learns from his wife that his son needs him, and he immediately goes to check on him. His son, Michael, is comfortable talking to him—another indicator of the closeness of their relationship. The situation in this chapter revolves around how to manage worry and concern. Sam leans on specific learnings from Stephen R. Covey's ***The 7 Habits of Highly Effective People***, originally published in 1990.

This TPAP "control over concern" elates to team formation in that new teams typically lack focus.

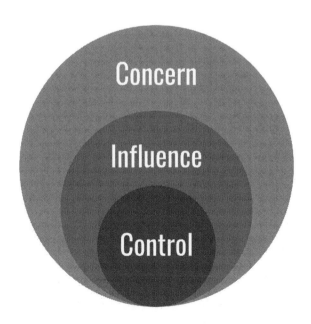

By acknowledging the circle of concern, you demonstrate empathy with where your team is starting, which then allows you to detail all the areas where they can still influence and control outcomes. Instilling this mindset in your team right from the start will allow you to generate quick wins, which will in turn reinforce the mindset, creating a virtuous circle of proactive behaviors. Once this discipline is mastered, you will experience far greater gains in productivity. Also, as a leader who embodies this philosophy, your modeling of the proactive mindset will positively affect your team's culture.

Key Takeaways:

- *Attitude is everything*: Each person can prevent concerns from dominating his or her day-to-day reality. To practice this principle, ask yourself (and your team) to observe reactions to receiving negative news and learn how to purposefully choose to maintain a neutral attitude. Then concentrate on what needs to happen to manage the situation.

- *Proactivity is divine*: Individuals can take charge of their life by understanding the three circles of their existence (concern, influence, control). Segmenting issues into influenceable and controllable buckets will make each team member (and therefore the team) more positive, productive, and effective.

- *Know thyself:* Humans experience the world from the inside out, which is why self-awareness is so crucial.

What are your negative emotional triggers? How can you mitigate them when they are stimulated? What does it take for you to glean the positive from the negative? Answering these types of questions will help you more effectively influence difficult internal states.

- *Three power words*: *Can* must win out over *can't*, *will* must dominate *won't*, and *do* must run circles around *don't* for you and your team to accomplish your goals. When you get the power of *can*, *will*, and *do* on your side, there is little that can stand in your path to success.

- *Fuggedaboutit*: If there is legitimately no action that can influence or change an outcome—move it into the circle of concern and then forget about it.

Applying this TPAP:

- Acknowledge feelings. A strong sense of uncertainty usually pervades new teams, despite their excitement and willingness to embark on the journey. Ignore these uncertain emotions at your own peril. A better approach is to directly address the elephants in the room by calling them out. Then help the team sort these uncertainties into true areas of concern (where no action will change anything) and areas where applying a bit of energy can either change a given outcome or at least mitigate a negative circumstance. Encouraging this type of openness in the early days of a team and providing a platform for such discussions will allow you to consistently re-focus everyone on what matters. (For tips on how to establish open communications with your team, visit https://elearn-academy. gr/9-secrets-creating-open-communication-workplace/).

- Embed proactivity as a core team philosophy. Early on, it is important to help your new team distinguish between the areas they fully control (and can be proactive about) and aspects of the work that are merely influenceable (and how to develop their ability to influence outcomes). As the leader, you should set the tone early and often and remain consistent while modeling the behavior you expect to see in others. Usually, the controllable areas relate to the three power words: *can*, *will*, and *do*. If an issue or task can be acted upon, it should be acted upon only to the degree that acting will advance the team's cause. If doing something resolves an issue or helps to complete a task, then it must be done. The more you encourage and reward your team for focusing on what's within their collective control, the more productive they will be. (For a simple reference on the circles of control, influence, and concern, visit https://bit.ly/2CYALsk).

- Play what-if. In ***Great by Choice***, Jim Collins and researchers identify productive paranoia as a critical behavior of companies who succeed in uncertain environments. Productive paranoia is the practice of regularly identifying the types of influenceable issues that could disrupt accomplishment of the mission and outlining mitigation strategies to be employed in the event of any of the issues occurring. Take time to review these types of issues, augment or edit the list, and assign persons in charge (PICs). Make this contingency plan easily accessible to all team members. Knowing that you have a plan for worst-case scenarios will allow your new team to focus without the fog of unnecessary worry.

Discussing this TPAP:

1. To what degree do you take the time to acknowledge the emotional state of your people as your team forms?

2. What are the biggest concerns on the minds of your people currently? To what degree will acting on these concerns change the impact or outcome?

3. How would you assess your team's spirit of proactivity vs. reactivity?

4. How often do you make time to consider worst-case scenarios as a team? How prepared are you for these scenarios?

5. What is your normal reaction to concerns? What do you need to change in your attitude to manage how you feel about concerns more effectively?

TPAP #3 – Serve and Support

In Chapter Four, Sam revisits one of his first major lessons as a leader—the moment he discovered that he abhorred the "boss" title. This realization led him to adopt a servant leader mindset. During a conversation with his wife, she referred to the typical organizational hierarchy as "Donkey-Konging" and implored Sam to invert the standard triangle and lead his people through challenges as opposed to being the challenger. The book referenced in this chapter is *The Servant: A Simple Story About the True Essence of Leadership* by James Hunter, which tells the story of a business executive who starts to lose his grip as a boss, husband, father, and coach. He goes on a week-long retreat at a Benedictine monastery to re-center and find his balance. During the retreat, a former Wall Street legend turned monk shows him a different perspective on leadership—servant leadership.

Servant leadership is key to accelerating team performance overall, but the sooner you adopt the principle of leading with authority versus power, the greater the degree of followership you will engender in your new staff. They will follow your directions not because of your title, but because they value their relationship with you. Power-based leadership is the ability to force or coerce people into action even if they don't believe in (or understand) the instructions. Servant leadership, in contrast, is the ability to get people to follow your direction because of your personal influence—regardless of your title.

Key Takeaways:

1. *Build trust and the rest will follow*: Leadership used to be about getting people to work for you because of the power of the position you held; in this model, title and number of direct reports reflected your leadership capability. In today's less hierarchical virtual business world, influencing others to follow you regardless of your positional power becomes far more critical. Building trust is the true ability of today's boundary-less power influencers.

2. *No Donkey-Konging!* Just as in the classic arcade game, you must decide whether you will direct your new team from the top as the "boss" (aka Donkey Kong), or as a collective Mario with the team goal of defeating Donkey Kong. Think about it from the point of view of your team, and the answer is apparent. Especially in the early stages of team formation, do you really want to be the one throwing flaming barrels at people as they're trying to move forward?

3. *Remember who's the boss*: In the inverted triangle model, the customer is number one, and therefore the employees tasked with creating value for the customer are the most important stakeholders in the organization. Everything you do as a leader should be in support of what your value creators require to succeed in their interactions with customers.

4. *Patience is divine*: A key component of servant leadership is the ability to control yourself and your reactions to disappointment. New teams are inherently fragile and

overly sensitive to your moods. Being quick with praise and taking personal responsibility for team failings will demonstrate to your burgeoning group the right way to handle stress.

Applying this TPAP:

The application ideas below are not something you can workshop or even something your team will overtly recall. What follows are behaviors that, when manifested, will increase your credibility and authority, ensuring that your new team follows your direction in the forming stage not because they must, but because they want to.

- Be trustworthy. There are five key behaviors you must consistently exhibit as a leader to create trust with your new team:
  - Humanity: See the individuals in your team as people first—not titles, functions, or head counts. Connect with each person on a human level, acknowledging that there is a world beyond the workplace that has a major impact on how people perform.
  - Authenticity: Keep it real by being transparent about your failings as much as your successes. Ensure that what people see is what they get, with no hidden agendas or politics.
  - Vulnerability: Demonstrate your imperfections and ask for help as needed. Make it clear that you do not

have all the answers. Reveal your comfort in your own skin. Create a culture of dealing with facts as they are, with no apologies.

- ○ Openness: Remain receptive to new ideas and approaches to problem solving. Inspire creativity, resist the status quo, and help your team look at problems from different angles without attacking one another. Leverage collaboration to make powerful connections between people.
- ○ Transparency: Be honest. Call it like you see it and value fairness and equity. Eliminate double standards. Eradicate unnecessary double-talk and political correctness and get to the heart of matters.

- Demonstrate servant leadership. Discuss the hierarchy of your organization with your team early on. Use the graphic below to visualize the concept that the customer is the top priority and that the company's value generators must be supported most of all. Then live the inverted triangle by working alongside your value creators as much as possible to let them know they have your full support. Interact with the direct customer frequently to ensure that your products and/or services are hitting the right notes with them.

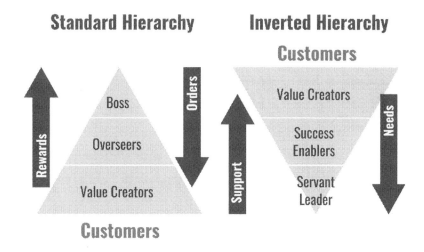

- Lead with love. In **_The Servant_**, authority is gained by sacrificing for those you lead. Yet there can be no service or sacrifice if there is no love (defined as the alignment between your intentions and your actions). As much as possible, look to embody the following qualities:
  - Patience – self-restraint
  - Humility – authenticity
  - Respect – live the "Golden Rule"
  - Selflessness – focus on meeting others' needs
  - Forgiveness – move on when disappointed
  - Commitment – consistency

Discussing this TPAP:

1. What are the benefits of adopting the servant leadership approach?

2. How significant of a change would it be for you to transform your leadership style?

3. To what degree do your people trust you? How do you know?

4. How vulnerable can you be with your team about your own failings and struggles?

5. What are the biggest current challenges faced by your front liners? What would be the impact of prioritizing and addressing these challenges? What is the cost of doing nothing?

TPAP #4 – Fill Buckets Daily

When we meet Sam Lombardi in Chapter One, we are introduced to a leader on the brink of a significant career change. There is a high degree of uncertainty, and this allows worry and negative thoughts to enter his mind. As he considers his advancing age, a bad habit (habitual lateness), and the recent termination of several colleagues, he begins to feel demoralized. Then he falls back on the learnings from ***How Full is Your Bucket?*** by Donald O. Clifton and Tom Rath.

How Full is Your Bucket? was first published in 2004 and remains as one of the top business and management books on Amazon.com. According to Clifton and Rath, studies show that organizational leaders who focus on maximizing employee strengths and share positive emotions have work groups with a more positive mood, enhanced job satisfaction, greater engagement, and improved performance. The key leadership concept is that the more praise and recognition a leader gives, the higher the team's engagement level, but also the better the attitude of the leader. This is essential in the forming stage of a team when members are most hungry for guidance and most likely to experience significant frustration due to lack of clarity.

Key Takeaways:

- *Mood matters*: You may or may not have heard of the phrase *Shadow of the Leader*. The shadow of the leader is basically the image and impression you leave in your interactions with your people. They are far more sensitive to the nuances of your mood than you might realize. While you shouldn't aim to project an air of false positivity, be conscious of the impact negative emotions have on your new team.

- *Sincerity sells*: The idea here is not to walk around giving half-hearted compliments and praise to your people. The key is to be so engaged with your team that you catch people doing things right often, and in these crucial moments you recognize and reward the behaviors you want every colleague to emulate.

- *Why so serious?* At the end of the day, you don't want work to ruin anyone's life—yours or anyone else's. Create a relaxed environment where people feel empowered and have the freedom to make decisions. Encourage laughter and comradery. Most people spend over half their lives working—to do that in a stifling environment is just not cool!

- *Dodge and weave*: No matter what you do as a leader, some people will leave your team looking for greener pastures. When you reflect on your relationship with these colleagues, you want to know that you did everything in your power to support, develop, and boost them. If you've done that, then you should be positive about their exits as well.

Applying this TPAP:

- Regularly assess yourself for positive impact (bucket filling). Leverage the resource at http://bit.ly/2XsRL1L to assess the impact you are having on those around you. If you answer no more than yes, you may need to adjust your behaviors. Ask for a second opinion from someone you trust to gain a realistic perspective on your interactions with others.

- Implement a mood meter. Your aim as the team is forming should be to infuse the group with positive, can-do energy. Start your regular staff meetings with a discussion of mood versus workload. Plot each team member's name on the grid (download here: http://bit.ly/2v73pmK) and utilize a specific bucket-filling strategy that week for each part of the mood meter.

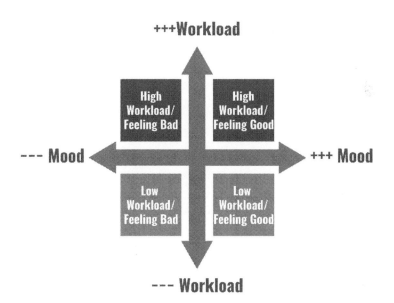

- Individualize recognition. During the onboarding process for each team member, be sure to ask them these questions (and then use their responses to personalize how you recognize them):
  - From whom do you most like to receive recognition or praise?
  - What type of recognition or praise do you like best? Do you like public, private, written, verbal, or other kinds of recognition?
  - What form of recognition motivates you the most? Do you like gift certificates, a title for winning a competition, a meaningful note or email, or something else?
  - What is the greatest recognition you have ever received?

- Reward regularly. Leverage expected and unexpected gifts and rewards to boost mood and motivation for your new team. Give smiles, praise, your time, and/or small tokens of your appreciation. Be sure to spread the love across your whole team—everyone does something brilliantly; it is up to you to catch them in the act and reward them accordingly. Amplify this culture by encouraging teammates to recognize one another for positive team contributions and behaviors.

Discussing this TPAP:

1. When assessing the performance of an employee, to what degree do you focus on and emphasize their strengths versus their weaknesses?

2. What are your natural mood boosters, and how do you ensure that you project a positive mood as much as possible?

3. To what degree do you recognize your people in the way that motivates them the most?

4. How often do you smile at work?

5. Have you praised a colleague today?

TPAP #5 – Keep Social Contracts

In Chapter Five, after their first successful business review, Sam and Jim take their team out for drinks at a local pub. Sam notices that despite how closely everyone works together, there still seem to be many things people don't know about one another. The team then bonds over structured and unstructured banter as relationships are cemented. The act of winning and celebrating together fuses the group into a more cohesive unit.

Informal team bonding (which is different from team building) can be a powerful catalyst to accelerate a team's formation when leveraged correctly. Timing is everything when it comes to using this tool. Social contracts are the informal, unwritten rules of the team; they are where the "soul" of the team comes to life. The creation of the first team norms may dictate how quickly you can progress through the other stages of storming, norming, and performing.

Key Takeaways:
- *Work for it*: Link informal team-bonding sessions to concrete business results. This strategy releases energy in the group by allowing their leader(s) to appreciate them in a laid-back setting.
- *Break the ice*: Keep a few good conversation starters handy to keep the dialogue flowing and ensure that all team members are engaged.
- *Keep it up*: Work to strike the right balance between

structured collaboration (work-related) and unstructured bonding (social contracting). Consistency is key, but so is frequency.

Applying this TPAP:

- Schedule it. Look at your key deliverables calendar and identify moments where, should your team perform to expectations, you will schedule some informal downtime. Some ideas for good informal bonding activities are beers, karaoke, mini golf, go-cart racing, escape rooms, poker, cooking classes, etc. The key is to let people know in advance that these activities are locked in, so you maximize attendance without your team members sacrificing equally valuable personal time.

- Reinforce the social contract. Informal team bonding is where the team's norms are often born. Pay attention to behaviors recognized as valuable by the team and those ridiculed and work to formalize these for team self-regulation. Make use of symbolic rewards related to the best use of positive norms and assess emblematic penalties for those who fail to meet the team's standards. Here's an example of a team social contract: http://bit.ly/2UKaPLI

Discussing this TPAP:

1. What are the key norms of your team? Which behaviors are routinely praised and which behaviors lead to the most conflict?
2. How can you formalize the behaviors that will lead to productive and engaging team interactions?
3. What are some key upcoming milestones you'd like to celebrate once they are achieved?
4. When is the last time you had informal downtime with your team?
5. Who can you empower on your team to ensure that team bonding happens on a regular basis?

SECTION II:

STORMING

Storming
6. **Raise Your Leadership Lid**
7. **Team DNA**
8. **Get The INNERview**
9. **WHY Before WHAT**
10. **Connect The Dots**

Executive Summary: Storming

Let's return to our basketball team analogy, shall we? You've been practicing and improving steadily, and the team has accumulated a few early wins. Your best players are delivering results, but the team is barely winning and has had some very close calls. Then the losses start piling up, and your coach calls an emergency team meeting. This meeting is far from constructive, with team members blaming one another for the recent spate of losses and no one taking responsibility for their actions. It's like everyone has forgotten the formula that led to the quick wins; some team members even question the coach's decision-making.

Welcome to the storming stage.

Although your group has made it through the tumultuous period of forming, cohesion has not yet cemented. Decisions likely do not come easily within the group. Team members vie for position as they attempt to establish themselves in relation to other team members. Clarity of purpose increases, but plenty of uncertainties persist. Cliques and factions form, and there may be power struggles. The team needs to focus on its goals to avoid being distracted by relationships and emotional issues. Compromises may be required in order to enable progress.

Conventional wisdom suggests that the role of the leader at this stage is to coach but coaching alone is not enough to bring a dysfunctional group through stormy seas with everyone intact. Your leadership capability will be tested most during this process, which is why it is essential to focus on raising your leadership lid (TPAP #6). Despite your resolve, it is your leadership acumen that determines your ability to influence the group to normalize toward more positive and productive behaviors. Understanding everyone's natural patterns of thinking, feeling, and behaving can be a true performance accelerator—especially when framed in the form of the Team DNA grid exercise (TPAP #7).

Still, you need to dig deeper than talent to expose the true *why* of each member of your team, and this is where **INNERviewing** (TPAP #8) becomes handy. The insights gained from **INNERviews** can then be collated into a greater purpose for your group once you apply the model of *why* before *what* (TPAP #9), which will imbue your team with a solid sense of purpose to rally behind despite the difficulties and challenges to come. When a team is storming, it is essential that you connect as well as communicate. Once again, this relates to connecting the dots (TPAP #10) between your team's purpose and the results you expect.

TPAP #6 – Raise Your Leadership Lid

At the end of Chapter Five, Sam realizes that Jim Kelly is a leader whose leadership acumen exceeds his own. This is an important realization for Sam, as it signals a shift in his relationship with Jim and increases his willingness to follow his new leader due to his authority and not his positional power. Jim exhibits several trust-building behaviors during the informal team-bonding session, first by communicating his "number" (the amount he'd need to leave Giant), and then with his open recognition and praise of Sam in front of the team, which confirms Sam's leadership ability in the same turn.

Leadership acumen is especially important once your team transitions from forming to storming. Anyone can bark orders; it is far more challenging to keep a group from coalescing into cliques and silos and/or losing focus due to relationship conflicts and emotional issues. If you detect the formation of cliques or the loss of focus, you must begin to shift your style from directing (telling the answer) to coaching (guiding toward the answers). What matters far more than your determination to succeed in this stage is your ability to keep your team focused on collective goals, improve group decision-making, and make the right compromises to enable progress.

As noted in Chapter Five, John C. Maxwell details the Law of the Lid in his publication *The 21 Irrefutable Laws of Leadership*. He argues that your effectiveness and impact as a leader are both largely determined by the figurative "height" of your leadership lid. If your leadership lid is low, so is your potential to lead and succeed, and vice versa. In this law, leadership capability acts as a success amplifier, augmenting effectiveness and impact.

Key Takeaways:

1. *Leadership is influence*: John C. Maxwell keeps the definition of leadership very simple. To measure your leadership ability, simply measure your influence. Want to improve your leadership ability? Learn how to augment your influence.

2. *Know your lid*: Self-knowledge and -awareness are critical for any leader. Are you consistently underachieving versus your own and others' expectations? Do people naturally gravitate toward you in groups? Understanding your starting point is key.

3. *Raise your lid*: Once you understand your starting point, consciously work to increase your leadership acumen by improving your ability to influence people and outcomes.

Applying this TPAP:

- Assess your leadership ability. There are a number of leadership-capability assessments available online, including one in ***The 21 Irrefutable Laws of Leadership***. Forbes.com also has a very useful and actionable assessment called "Think You're a Leader? Take the Test and Find Out." This assessment allows you to rate yourself on a scale of on to ten against criteria such as character, vision, strategy, tactics, focus, and persuasiveness, among others. Visit http://bit.ly/2GutbrB to take the assessment online.

- Potentialize your leadership strengths. Select the area where you scored the highest on the assessment and ask yourself the following questions:
    - When was the last time I used this leadership area to successfully influence people or an outcome?
    - What steps did I take to achieve this outcome?
    - How can I use this leadership area more consistently?

- Minimize your leadership gaps. Select the area where you scored the lowest on the assessment and ask yourself the following questions:
    - What is preventing me (knowledge, experience, skills) from leveraging this area more effectively?
    - What steps should I take to begin to improve in this leadership area?

- Repeat with each successive strength and weakness until you have maximized each leadership strength area and elevated each leadership weakness area.

Discussing this TPAP:

1. To what degree do you think that further developing your leadership capabilities will augment your effectiveness?

2. Who are the most difficult members of your team to influence? In what area do you need to elevate your leadership skills to more effectively influence them?

3. To what degree are you directing your team versus coaching them?

4. How do you manage failure: blame your team or blame yourself?

5. How readily do you ask for help when confronted with difficulty?

TPAP #7 – Team DNA

In Chapter Six, despite having a full team with some established norms (nicknames, lunches as a team), Sam learns that all is not well with his group. Specifically, it appears that despite clear direction in terms of who should be doing what based on roles, there is misalignment with what people want to do and what each person does best. After taking the Clifton Strengths® assessment, Sam enlists the help of team-building consultant Missy Richards to bridge the gap. He is quite intrigued with the core philosophy of strengths-based management, which posits that breakout performance is achieved faster by investing in strengths rather than fixing weaknesses.

In the storming stage, it is typical for team members to vie for position as they attempt to establish themselves in relation to other team members. Rather than collaborating for greater synergies and productivity, teams in this stage compete amongst themselves. Sometimes this is driven by lack of role clarity, or in the case of Sam's team, individual preferences and natural talents make it clear that some people's roles have been improperly assigned. To break through this barrier, tools like Clifton Strengths® or other such personality assessments can be useful to help team members better relate to one another and the tasks at hand.

Where the Clifton Strengths® differentiates itself from other assessments, however, is in the Team DNA grid (introduced in ***Strengths Based Leadership***). This grid is one of the most powerful team management resources available and can power a group through the storming stage. The grid contains several key pieces of information, including:

- Which team members are dominant in each of the four domains of strength (executing, influencing, relationship building, strategic thinking)
- Team talents (top five signature talents of your team)
- Team blind spots (domains with the lowest overall concentration of talents represented)
- Outliers (individuals on the team with talents no one else possesses)

Key Takeaways:
- *See the person, not the role*: We often hire people with specific experience for certain roles. But this practice may limit team potential. By digging to understand everyone's unique talents and strengths, we can discover other unconventional ways to motivate and inspire individual and team performance.
- *Talent does not equal strength (in fact, it may be a weakness)*: After taking the Clifton Strengths® assessment, you are gifted with your top five *talent* themes. *Talent* is defined as a naturally recurring pattern of thinking, feeling, and behaving that can be productively applied. *Weakness* is defined as a talent that is not being productively applied and that might be adversely

impacting both the individual and others.

- *Convince the skeptics*: One of the more difficult concepts to get across to someone in a senior position (and who is therefore already successful) is that they can accelerate or consolidate their success by investing time in learning more about their talents and working to turn them into strengths. Gallup provides a number of useful tools for deeper self-reflection, as well as the services of a legion of coaches who can properly engage your executives and demonstrate that, even for them, there is room to grow.
- *Phone a friend*: If you want to embark on a team DNA assessment, follow Sam's example and call in a Certified Strengths Coach. Strengths-based management is deceptively simple on the surface, but far deeper than you may fully appreciate just by reading a few of the books and taking the assessments.
- *DNA must be visible to be tangible*: Gallup's language of talent and strengths is new to most people, and it might take some time before these concepts become second nature. To accelerate the momentum from a team strengths workshop, make sure each team member's top five theme is visible always, and the team strengths grid accessible to all team members.

Applying this TPAP:
- Find the right tool for you. Clifton Strengths® is one of a series of available tools that assess personality and

provide deeper insight into individual motivations and behaviors. For is a comparison of Clifton Strengths® and Myers-Briggs, visit http://bit.ly/2VQtT7P.

- Hire an expert. Unless you are a Certified Strengths Coach or have some other type of team facilitation expertise or certification, it is highly recommended that you invest in an expert who can design a program tailored to the specific needs of your team. You can find a directory of US-based certified Strengths Coaches here: http://bit. ly/2VQtT7P. Any consultant worth their fee will start the process by assessing your needs and finding out more about the personalities involved and specific goals and challenges of your team.

- Lead by example. Fully participate in all aspects of the team building, from the assessments to the discussions. Usually, these activities provide opportunities for the team leader (you) to receive anonymous feedback from the team about the impact your leadership style has on the group. Remain open-minded, do not get defensive, and take the feedback as the gift it is. Commit to act on what you hear.

- Remove hierarchy from the equation. The essence of exploring team DNA is identifying your team leaders regardless of rank or tenure. The Clifton Strengths® assessment and team DNA grid will allow you to quickly spot your execution, influencing, relationship-building, and strategic-thinking experts. Once you start relying on teammates as leaders in their respective areas, their sense of empowerment will multiply and so will your productivity!

- Don't allow the whirlwind to unglue your team. The first few days and weeks after a good team-building session are the most critical. When the euphoria of the "Kumbaya" moment has passed and people get busy again, all that they learned and committed to do goes out the window. It is your job to implant and reinforce new team norms as soon as you get back to the office and remain consistent in order to embed these norms into the fabric of your group. Make the lessons visible by printing team top five reports and DNA grids and requesting that each team member post theirs somewhere easily accessible and visible. Incorporate the language of talent and strengths into your team's lexicon. For more information on the value of building a strengths-based team visit http://bit.ly/2v73MOa and visit http://bit.ly/2vcXo8a for some articles on building a strengths-based organization.

Discussing this TPAP:
1. How well do you understand the unique talents, strengths, and skills of each of your team members as well as the collective talents, strengths, and skills of

the group as a whole?

2. To what degree are your expectations of a team members' performances aligned with their natural talents, strengths, and skills?

3. What are the potential powerful partnerships inherent in your team that could be maximized by better understanding what each person brings to the table in terms of strengths?

4. What are the potential blind spots of your team—areas where there is not a high degree of natural talent, strength, and/or skills?

5. What return can you expect by focusing on augmenting your team's natural talents, strengths, and skills versus trying to fix your team's weaknesses?

TPAP #8 – Get the INNERview

As the story progresses to Chapter Seven, Sam's team starts to coalesce but productivity is slow to manifest. Sam realizes how difficult it is to embed learnings from team building once "real life" restarts. He seeks counsel from his mentor, Logan Dunn, who asks a provocative question: how well do you *really* know your team members?

Sam consults with Dave and Rob, and they come up with a strategy to better understand each team member's unique motivators, performance detractors, and preferred recognition types. Over the course of a week they conduct **INNERviews** with each team member. Through this process, they gain a deeper understanding of their team story and ultimately arrive at greater clarity in their collective mission.

Team storming requires a strong coaching aspect from you, the leader. You are required to go beyond skills, roles, and talents; uncover drives and barriers; and praise preferences. Investing your time in this process has a triple impact: first, it demonstrates your desire to really get to know your people on a deeper level; second, this knowledge can be leveraged to more effectively coach and inspire great performance; and finally, from your collective narrative you can more readily tap into your team's purpose. In-depth knowledge of your people is power!

Key Takeaways:

1. *Everyone needs a coach*: Notice how Sam turns to mentors and experts throughout his journey to build a high-performance team. He acknowledges that he doesn't have all the answers and is open to challenging his own conventions in pursuit of the greater goal.

2. *Skip this step at your own peril*: You may be asking yourself at this point—how necessary is it to spend time digging further into the background of your people? Depending on the size of your group, the task can seem daunting. But you need these people to perform for you, and investing this time in the storming stage will save you significant time later.

3. *Consistency is key*: Make sure that you ask each team member the same set of questions so you can easily compare the responses to find patterns.

Applying this TPAP:

- Design your **INNERview**. In this process, as in life, asking the right questions goes a long way. It's important that you are comfortable with the questions, so take some time to decide how you will navigate the **INNERview**. In Chapter Seven, Sam asks the following questions:
  - What name do you prefer to be called? (motivators)
  - When is your birthday? Are birthdays important to you? (motivators)
  - Tell me more about your family background. What

do your parents do for work? How many siblings do you have? What do they do? (values)

○ What were some key turning points in your life that made you the person you are today? (values)

○ What do you really love about your work? (motivators)

○ What drives you crazy about your work? (detractors)

○ Did you expect to be doing this kind work at this time in your life? (motivators)

○ What attributes do you value in your best friends? (values)

○ What has been the highlight of your life so far? (values, motivators, recognition)

○ What do you most regret about your life? (detractors)

○ How do you want people to view you? (motivators)

○ When do you feel the most pride about your work? (motivators)

○ When you achieve success at work, how do you like to be recognized? (motivators, recognition)

These questions begin by addressing general topics, then progress to touch on deeper levels of self-awareness and aspiration. Here is a template you can download for use and re-use: http://bit.ly/2GtkZHR.

- Schedule it. Like most things in life, if we don't put it on the calendar, it doesn't happen. Set aside a block of time to conduct the **INNERviews**. Allocate at least one hour per conversation to ensure that all the questions get answered. Then allocate another two to three hours to compile the responses into a single document. Here is an easy template you can download for use and re-use.

- Break the ice. It's important that your colleague understands that the purpose of the conversation is to help you get to know them better. Adopt a collegial tone and stress that this isn't a boss-employee dialogue, but more of a person-to-person conversation. No matter how long you've been working with someone, chances are there are many things you still don't know about them. Start with a few easy questions to set the tone and be prepared to ask follow-up questions if the answers are not totally clear.

- Reciprocate. In addition to sharing what you've learned with your teammate, find time to let them **INNERview** *you*. Then compare your answers to build a powerful partnership.

Discussing this TPAP:
1. How well do you know each of your team members on a fundamental level?
2. How well do each of your team members know you on a fundamental level?
3. Collectively, what inspires and motivates your team?
4. Do you have a coach or mentor you can turn to for advice and counsel?

TPAP #9 – WHY before WHAT

The other key lesson of Chapter Seven emerges from the discussion Sam and Logan have about the military's use of basic training to impose a high-performance culture. After Sam, Dave, and Rob identify the patterns in the **INNERview** responses, they arrive upon the key elements that bond the team together, which then form the basis of the culture they wish to manifest. From the team's collective narratives, they can clearly define their mission. Once the *why* is clear, developing the *how* and *what* is a straight-line exercise.

One of the principal symptoms of a team in the storming stage is the persistence of uncertainty that can lead to power struggles amongst team members. This lack of clarity can be eliminated via implementing some of the principles recommended for use during the forming stage, but every team also needs a clear reason to exist—a cause or set of beliefs to rally behind. Once this *why* is defined, it's much easier to keep the group aligned and focused on the controllable and influenceable issues and actions before them. Achievement of goals becomes much easier when the link between the mission and the enabling culture is explicit and encompasses the intangible qualities for which you've hired and onboarded.

Why can be defined using the Hedgehog Concept from *Good to Great* by Jim Collins. This crucial business theory was derived from analyzing good to great companies and discovering that each of these high-performing companies transformed their business by crystallizing their core reason for being—as evidenced by the first question in the Hedgehog Concept: "What are you *deeply* passionate about?"

Deep passion has long been a driver of leader companies and leader individuals, but it must be matched by clear competency. This is where the next question—"What can you be best in the world at?"—comes in. The final question completes the focus of the company, team, or individual—"What drives your economic engine?" Deep understanding and alignment between the company's purpose, capabilities, and profit drivers define success for good to great companies. Still, the *why* always comes first because, as Simon Sinek states in **Start with Why**, "People don't buy what you do, they buy *why* you do it."

Key Takeaways:

1. *Crystallize your passion*: Why do you get out of bed every morning? What are you fighting for? What inspires you to be your absolute best? Answering these sorts of questions and aligning the responses as a team can help make your beliefs concrete. The more solid your team's beliefs, the easier it will be to align your cause with *what* you need to do to make it real.

2. *Claim what you can*: The second hedgehog question asks, "What *can* you be best in the world (industry, company) at?" The key is to be as realistic as possible when answering this question. Once you know what you

can be best at, then claim it as the second component of your *why*. Obviously, it is of equal importance to recognize that which you *cannot* be best at as well.

3. *The X factor*: Great companies boil their business down to one key metric, defined as sales (or profits or margins) per X. With the right Key Performance Indicator (KPI), exponential growth becomes a matter of discipline and focus.

Applying this TPAP:

- Know yourself and your team. Leverage resources like these offered by Simon Sinek to find your *why*. Conduct exercises (like the **INNERviews** described in Chapter Seven) to document the values, motivators, and detractors for your team. Mine the data gathered for congruence and ask yourself the following questions:
  - What is our origin story?
  - What do we all have in common from a values perspective?
  - What is the consistent theme in our motivators?
  - What are the things that detract us from doing our best?

The responses will point you in the direction of deep passion. Don't rely on the corporate mission unless you can confirm that it truly ignites a fire to be the best in your team. Test the new *why* statement with your team for clarity and reaction. The *why* statement should be the kind of thing that energizes you and your team at a glance, so it's critical to get it right.

- Find your team's true capability: We live in a world that tells us we are supposed to be well rounded, but the most successful individuals and companies are far from well rounded—in fact, they are usually quite gifted in a beautifully specific way. To further narrow down your true capability, you need to conduct a success inventory. Revisit the **INNERview** outputs and *why* statements, and you will gain a glimpse into a capability trend. Usually the things we love to do are also things at which we have enjoyed some degree of success. SWOT analysis is a simple way to begin to clarify core competencies:

Strengths	Weaknesses
What are your strengths?	What are your weaknesses?
What do you do better than your competitors?	What do your competitors do better than you?
What can you improve given the current situation?	What can you improve given the current situation?
What do others perceive as your strengths?	What do others perceive as your weaknesses?

Objective of Venture

	What trends or conditions may negatively impact you?
What trends or conditions may positively impact you?	What are your competitors doing that may impact you?
What opportunities are available to you?	Do you have solid financial support?
	What impact do your weaknesses have on the threats to you?
Opportunities	**Threats**

- Pick the KPI in the haystack. What distinguished the *Good to Great* companies from their comparison set was that they anguished over identifying the single key performance indicator (KPI) that would define their business model. Here's an example of what that might look like for a publishing company: Traditional book publishers think in terms of sales per author or sales per book published, but what if the KPI was sales per reader? Can you see how redefining the KPI would drive different actions from the publisher? If profit per author is the success metric, then the way to achieve exponential growth is either to have a phenomenal suite of authors who consistently put out great content or a few superstar authors who have legions of fans (or both). However, if the measure of success is profit per reader, then the publishing company's focus changes significantly. Now, the company needs to focus on building its own brand so that no matter who the author is, readers buy the book anyway.

There is no one right way to define the right measuring stick for your team. Trial and error (and lots of internal debate) is the only way to get there. RhythmSystems.com has compiled a helpful list of examples. The key is to pick the metric that most aligns with your *why* and *how* and then stick to it with dogged discipline.

Discussing this TPAP:

1. To what degree is your team purpose driven or task driven?

2. How well do you currently understand the collective inspirations, motivators, and underlying values of your team?

3. How would you articulate the culture of your team— the shared values, norms, and objectives that bind the group together?

4. What are the areas where it is possible for your team to continuously achieve peak success based on previous experience and current areas of passion and capability?

5. What may need to change in how you are defining success for your team?

TPAP #10 – Connect the Dots

Back in Chapter Five, Sam's newly formed team faces their first major challenge—the business review with senior management. Sam understands this arena well and can effectively lead his team through the exercise, even though they are just getting to know each other. The key to his success in this early stage is his ability to go beyond merely communicating what needs to be done. He successfully connects the dots between the quality of the business review and the continued empowerment and trust of his team.

Power struggles are one of the defining characteristics of teams in the storming stage. In Chapter Five, the team is rife with internal conflict, but Sam leads them through by aligning everyone behind a common goal. He leverages his own unique strength in communication to positively influence and coax a great performance out of his young team.

This concept is explored in great depth in John C. Maxwell's book *Everyone Communicates, Few Connect.* Connecting is dependent on your ability to identify with people and relate to them. According to Maxwell, there are five key principles of connection:

- Connecting increases your influence.
- Connecting always focuses on others.
- Connecting goes beyond mere words.
- Connecting always requires energy.
- Connecting is an acquired skill, not a talent.

By increasing influence, focusing on others, painting clear images of success, energizing people, and constantly improving you can more effectively move a group through the storming stage. To effectively coach, you must first connect. Connect your leadership strengths and gaps to team challenges; connect to your team's DNA; connect on a deeply personal level via **INNERviews**; and connect the narrative of your group to your reason for being. Once all these dots are connected, you have a group primed for the norming stage.

Key Takeaways:

1. *Identify superordinate goals*: One well-established theory of group bonding is that people tend to coalesce faster when they are faced with common external challenges—in other words, in situations where they need one another to succeed. As Ron Friedman states in ***The Best Place to Work***, "It's easier to connect with someone when it's clear you're both on the same side and neither of you can succeed alone."

2. *Tell a good story*: Group norms are cemented in the myths that surround a team's struggles to succeed. Return to these myths early and often to remind your group of how far you all have come, challenges you all have overcome, and how you all have won despite significant obstacles.

3. *Ensure alignment*: It's more important to align on 70 percent of a plan and move forward than to fight

over the remaining 30 percent and never achieve total agreement. Think of alignments as critical milestones that must be conquered on the journey to full engagement.

Applying this TPAP:

- Increase your connecting acumen. Because connecting is a learned skill, it is important to assess yourself against the capability of great connectors. Identify your current strong points and work to solidify them. Then work to mitigate any glaring gaps. *Everyone Communicates, Few Connect* provides the following list of the attributes of true connectors:
  - They have strong relationships.
  - They are insightful.
  - They are successful.
  - They own their unique abilities.
  - They have made sacrifices.
  - They possess self-confidence.
  - They are authentic and have high integrity.
  - They are prepared to contribute.
  - They have a sense of humor.
  - They focus on others.
  - They are friends and advisors.

- Become a mythmaker. Start to think of your team goals in the context of quests. Your purpose plays a major role in the mission you are trying to achieve as a group. Visualize this goal for your group and talk about the various obstacles and challenges you can expect to encounter along your journey. Align on contingency plans in the event you face these barriers. And, as you conquer challenges, cement these as part of the legend of the team. Encourage the telling of these stories often to remind yourselves of what you are capable. Finally, turn your teammates into the heroes of their own quests by recognizing and rewarding them for individual victories and group accomplishments. The book ***Believe Me*** by Michael Margolis is a good resource for how to become a great mythmaker.

- Document your alignments. In Chapter Five, Rebecca introduces the concept of Fist to Five to the group as a way to share and capture group alignment and consensus. When a group is storming, decisions don't come easily, so building alignment is critical to achieving any progress. Introduce an easy alignment method into your team. Fist to Five works quite simply—upon the conclusion of a given topic, you ask the group if they agree on the next actions by signaling from fist (complete disagreement) to five (complete agreement). If anyone does not completely agree (four or lower), ask them why and work to provide enough clarity to get them to a five. The point here is that the group feels they have been heard and that any disagreements are publicly shared so they can be addressed.

Discussing this TPAP:

1. What are your connecting strengths and gaps?
2. To what degree are all the dots connected between your team's relationships, strengths, purpose, objectives, potential obstacles, and agreed-upon actions?
3. To what degree does your team have common external challenges that everyone is aligned in overcoming?
4. How can you transform your team's mission and everyday actions into a compelling narrative that connects the contributions of each team member to the overarching objective?
5. What methods can you employ to ensure that everyone on your team is aligned to key objectives and actions?

SECTION III:

NORMING

Norming

11. Enhance Team Trust
12. Encourage Productive Conflict
13. Enforce Commitments
14. Exercise Shared Accountability
15. Execute Until Achievement

Executive Summary: Norming

Now your basketball team is on a winning streak. The coach has everyone on the same page. Your starters are performing like stars, everyone understands the offensive and defensive schemes, and disagreements are handled amicably and productively. There is a general sense of empowerment amongst your group, and you experience more smiles than frowns. People have the capacity to do more.

This is what norming feels like.

Once you have conquered the seas of storming, agreement and consensus among team members become easier to achieve. Roles and responsibilities are clear and accepted. Big decisions are made by group agreement, and smaller decisions may be delegated to individuals or small teams within the group. Commitment and unity are strong as the team regularly engages in fun and social activities. The team discusses and develops its processes and working style and demonstrates the ability to express criticism constructively.

Some may feel that the key function of the leader in this stage is to facilitate and enable, but the true role of a leader with a norming team is to remain vigilant. There are often elements of team dysfunction that, if unaddressed, can drag the group back into the chaos of storming. Your role is that of a building inspector—ensuring that the foundations are solidly in place. Your most useful tool in this stage comes in the form of the framework developed by Patrick Lencioni in

The Five Dysfunctions of a Team.

The base of this foundation is enhanced trust (TPAP #11), for without real trust among team members, a feeling of invulnerability may pervade, setting you up for a precipitous fall. The next area to assess is harmony. If you have a team that avoids conflict, this false harmony will ensure goals and roles remain ambiguous. Your job is to encourage productive conflict (TPAP #12), in which issues are debated openly before commitments are made. Once outcomes and roles are aligned, you must root out all ambiguity and enforce commitments (TPAP #13). Avoid the "meeting after the meeting" syndrome.

Norms should ensure that everyone is held equally accountable for delivering against aligned plans (TPAP #14). The final step in inspecting to ensure you have truly normed as a group is to scrutinize the degree to which your team measures itself by achievement of collective results versus status and ego. This phase will require you to remain maniacally disciplined and to keep executing until goals are achieved (TPAP #15). Getting through the norming stage ultimately requires you to maintain a mindset of high diligence and rugged persistence.

TPAP #11 – Enhance Team Trust

During team building in Chapter Six, Sam and his team uncover an issue related to trust – they need to do more active listening, engage each other with sensitivity and positive intent, and enhance shared values and norms. After this realization, Sam and his team leaders are very intentional about cultivating trust, respect, sensitivity, and clear shared values. The **INNERviews**, social contracting, team nicknames, dartboard in Dave's office, and leader board are all tools leveraged to encourage openness and vulnerability among teammates—the cornerstones of trust.

After the chaos of team storming, norming feels like finding land after months adrift at sea with nothing but your will and wits to survive. The commitment and unity in the group is palpable and invigorating. However, you still need to inspect your expectations, and the starting point is examining the openness of your team. To examine trust effectively, you must understand what it means in the context of team norming.

Trust is defined as the consistent demonstration of shared team values, comprised of transactional continuums based on past behavior related to communications, competence, and contracts (i.e. doing what one commits to do on time and in full). In *Trust and Betrayal in the Workplace*, Dennis and Michelle Reina define **communication trust**, or trust of disclosure, as dependent upon the following:

- Telling the truth
- Admitting mistakes
- Giving and receiving constructive feedback
- Maintaining confidentiality
- Sharing information
- Speaking with good purpose.

Competence trust is related to trust of others' capability, and is demonstrated as follows:

- Respecting people's knowledge, skills, and abilities
- Respecting people's judgment
- Involving others and seeking their input
- Helping people learn skills.

Contractual trust is related to trust of character, and is shown by:

- Honoring agreements
- Encouraging mutually serving intentions
- Acting consistently
- Managing expectations
- Establishing boundaries.

The telltale sign that your team may have some trust issues is that there is a sense of invulnerability that pervades the group. This basically means that no one admits mistakes. If you detect this we're all perfect syndrome chances are high that you are experiencing team dysfunction that must be addressed. Other signs (as described in ***The Five Dysfunctions of a Team***) include:

- Hesitation to ask for help or provide constructive feedback
- Hesitation to offer help outside team members' own areas of responsibility
- Jumping to conclusions about the intentions and aptitudes of others without attempting to clarify them
- Failing to recognize and tap into one another's skills and experiences
- Wasting time and energy managing behaviors for effect
- Holding grudges
- Dreading meetings and finding reasons to avoid spending time together.

Addressing issues of trust must be prioritized, because if trust is not there then team cohesion is not possible. The stickiness of a team starts first with trust, which enables productive conflict, which increases commitment, which is assessed by shared accountability, which occurs to the degree that your team exhibits trust-building behaviors in a virtual circle of trust.

Applying this TPAP:

- Quantify the degree of the issue. Before you move into actions, you must first understand the degree and nature of your team's trust issues. Is distrust pervasive across the entire team or isolated in pockets of invulnerability? Patrick Lencioni provides an assessment tool for trust in ***The Five Dysfunctions of a Team*** that you can download here: http://bit.ly/2KWUeQi

- Identify the root cause. Leveraging the five *whys* approach, dig below the surface with your team to identify the root cause of your team's trust deficiency. Listen intently in this stage and validate your assumptions with brutal facts. It's important to act on the root cause, as misdirected actions may not address the underlying problem.

- Conduct a vulnerability exercise. I'm not suggesting you fall off a picnic table into the waiting arms of your group and ask your team to do the same. One of the hidden benefits of Clifton Strengths® for teams is that just as everyone has unique talents and strengths, so do they by default have areas of lesser talent. There is an exercise called *Love, Crazy, Envy* that is useful in getting people to admit what they love about their talents, what drives people crazy about them, and talents of others that they wished they possessed. Download the worksheet here: http://bit.ly/2Uph82f. The key benefit of this workshop is getting each person to appreciate themselves and gain greater appreciation for their teammates. If you have not conducted the Clifton Strengths® assessment with your team, you can download this team effectiveness workshop from the Table Group here: http://bit.ly/2IHgECK

Discussing this TPAP:
1. In which of the "three dimensions of trust" (character, communication, capability) do you need the most improvement as a team?

2. How would your team rate you in these "three dimensions of trust"?

3. How do you assess the current degree of openness of your team—defined as people's willingness to admit mistakes?

4. What are the root causes for your team's current trust gaps?

5. What trust-building interventions do you need to action on an individual and team level?

TPAP #12 – Encourage Productive Conflict

In Chapter Nine, as his team prepares for the final business review before the launch of Goltur, Sam notices that something has changed with how his team behaves in meetings. He perceives a lack of order in how everyone is jumping into the discussion as they passionately debate the right flow for the big presentation. Dave sets him straight by explaining that sometimes only through debate can you get enough viewpoints on the table to make the right decision. Sam then uses his newfound knowledge in the business review to gain more input in order to improve their pricing proposal for Goltur.

A team's norm, agreement and consensus is largely formed among the team when no one holds back their thoughts or feelings in meetings, and no one holds grudges or takes comments personally. To assess the degree of true alignment on your team, you need to assess the quality of your debates. In some instances, you will need to be the spark plug triggering people to engage on a given issue.

You may be thinking, *But what about all that positive advice about filling people's buckets (TPAP #3)?* Being a leader can sometimes be a delicate tightrope walk between nurturing, directing, encouraging, coaching, challenging, and empowering. Nowhere is this more evident than in knowing when and how to escalate conflict on your team and when and how to de-escalate conflict. The answer lies in whether the conflict is likely to result in a productive business outcome.

Productive business outcomes are those that advance and progress your team's cause, get you over roadblocks, and make all elements of a given situation clearer. However, there are right and wrong ways to unearth conflicts. The right way involves examining causes of conflict, not symptoms, through effective inquiry methods. Productive conflict requires willingness to be vulnerable, demonstration of sensitivity and candor, and skillful probing and validation.

Imagine witnessing the following dialogue in a team meeting between Mark, Kim, and their manager, Kwame.

Kim: "So that's the plan. If there are no further questions, I can start assigning roles…"

Mark: "Sorry, Kim, but the part about the pink elephant makes absolutely no sense. The data seems cherry-picked, and your recommendations don't consider the fact that pink elephants don't actually exist!"

Kwame: "Okay, Mark, clearly you have some strong opinions about the pink elephant section. Thanks for sharing. Kim, would you mind going over your assumptions related to the pink elephant one more time so we all clearly understand your recommendations?"

Kim: "Sure thing. Before I start, Mark, would you mind clarifying which data you feel is cherry-picked?"

In this example, Mark is not afraid of creating a conflict. However, his choice of words could easily derail the dialogue into an emotional argument about the quality of Kim's work, which she may take personally. Sensing this, Kwame de-escalates the emotional tenor of the dialogue by acknowledging Mark's concern and then softening and translating Mark's feedback into something Kim can digest and respond to. Kim also practices a conflict de-escalation technique by requesting clarity from Mark.

In this scenario, if Mark and Kim don't have trust between them, de-escalation may be impossible. But Kim and Kwame understand that while Mark may be a bit blunt, underneath the bluntness is a valuable query that makes this confrontation work. By translating, probing, softening, and clarifying, they will arrive at the underlying cause for Mark's concern, and by addressing the pink elephant in the room, they will achieve greater buy-in and alignment.

Applying this TPAP:
- Assess listening capability. One of the things that can take productive conflict south is colleagues who don't actively listen. Before effective debate can happen on a team, each person must commit to some key listening principles outlined in ***How to Communicate with Diplomacy and Tact***, a Dale Carnegie course:
  - Maintain eye contact with the person talking
  - Observe body language for incongruent messages
  - Don't interrupt, finish the speaker's sentence, or change the subject
  - Listen with empathy and for understanding

- ○ Clarify any uncertainties
- ○ Don't jump to conclusions or make assumptions
- ○ Remove all distractions and minimize bias
- ○ Try to see things from the speaker's perspective

Based on the list above, appoint an observer to comment on the quality of the team's listening skills after every meeting. Provide corrective feedback to the serial offenders and positive feedback to those demonstrating the desired behaviors.

- Find the sweet spot. Effective debate comes down to the degree of confidence of the debaters. According to Dale Carnegie, there is a continuum of communication from passive to aggressive, where confidence is the sweet spot between the two.

Passive	Confident	Aggressive
Concerned about others to the point of personal detriment	Will stand up for own rights, while sensitive to others	Self-centered
Stressed internally, though it may not show	Deals with stressful situations and moves on	Often is stressed and stresses others
Often manifested as a result of poor self-esteem	Requires a strong self-image	Often manifested as a result of poor self-esteem
Indirect and often not honest with self	Direct, honest, appropriate communication	Direct to point of inappropriateness
Often liked, but may not be respected	Often respected by others	May not be liked or respected
Builds others up even at own expense	Builds others up	Puts others down
Holds self accountable, but not others	Willing to take personal responsibility for own actions and hold others accountable	Holds other accountable but not self
Avoids confrontation, often overly apologetic	Tends to lead by example, does not seek nor avoid confrontation	Seeks confrontation, forces others to follow
Strict guidelines for self, but not others	Flexible with guidelines	Restrictive
Reserved, indirect, restrained	Open, yet sensitive, polite	Verbally abrasive
Avoids expressing feelings	Direct, but considerate	Extremely direct, forces feelings, thoughts, and ideas on others
Wishes	Asks	Demands

Have your team assess themselves on the communication-style continuum and then ask for validation by others who work closely with them. Once again, leverage your meeting observer to comment on the nature of team debates—passive, just right, or aggressive. Feedback is the key to improvement.

- Manage unproductive conflict effectively. Conflict in the workplace becomes unproductive when things turn personal or when conflict resolution styles inevitably clash. According to the *Harvard Business Review*, there are two types of conflict styles—avoiders and seekers— and there are four steps to analyzing and ultimately resolving specific conflicts: understanding the perspective of the other, assessing the form of conflict, deciding on an outcome, and then acting accordingly. Proactive team leaders realize that conflicts between teammates will arise eventually and pre-empt these conflicts by educating the group in advance of issues via workshopping, collective reading, and even role-playing scenarios. Visit http:// bit.ly/2IoAnHK for a resource on conflict modes, here for a resource from the *Harvard Business Review* on defining conflict styles, and http://bit.ly/2Ivo3pg for a free course on Conflict Resolution Foundations from LinkedIn Learning.

Discussing this TPAP:
   1. What percentage of your team typically engages (speaks openly and debates) on topics you consider to be business critical?

2. How often do you debate issues as a team?

3. How well do you understand the conflict resolution styles of yourself and your team?

4. What are the conflicts currently undermining your team's progress?

5. What is the impact of waiting until after conflict occurs to equip your team with the capabilities to effectively manage conflict?

TPAP #13 – Enforce Commitments

While Sam is recovering from his emergency knee surgery in Chapter Eight, something miraculous is happening on his team due to Dave's leadership and infectious influence. They begin gamifying cross-functional commitment through a team Leader Board, which links the Clifton Strengths® domains with time-bound deliverables. This new process not only infects the team with a rhythm of delivering, it also incentivizes delivery. Once he fully understands the mechanism, it's no wonder Sam is so impressed with how the team has progressed in his absence!

A clear signal that your team is norming can be seen in the way your group discusses and develops its processes and working style. This evolution of the social contract discussed in TPAP #5, where team commitment to ways of working become cemented. Commitment is all about clarity in expectations, behaviors, and deliverables. The enemies of commitment (as defined in **The Five Dysfunctions of a Team**) are the need for complete harmony and the requirement of full clarity.

Patrick Lencioni writes that teams that fail to commit:

- Are unprecise about course of action and urgencies
- Overanalyze to the point of missing opportunities
- Are scared to take necessary risks
- Fail to decide and move into actions
- Allow lack of absolute consensus to derail progress.

Teams that commit, in contrast:

- Create clarity on courses of action and urgencies
- Align on shared goals
- Fail forward by learning from errors
- Achieve first mover advantage versus the competition
- Have a bias toward action
- Remain flexible and adaptable in order to make necessary course corrections.

Applying this TPAP:

- Create clarity. It's impossible to commit and buy in if you don't understand the *why*s, *how*s, and *what*s of a given decision or course of direction. Leverage the power of *why* by explaining key rationales and then asking members of the team to play back what they have heard. This repetition will help ensure that the group "gets it." If your group is unable to clearly explain the basis for a commitment, then work to simplify your message into its raw essence. You don't need consensus, but you do need alignment and buy-in. This comes from allowing key voices to be heard on a given subject, providing relevant clarifications, and then moving forward to deciding. Another point to note here: If you as the leader are unclear, then make sure you recognize that reality without allowing the uncertainty to paralyze the team from moving forward, albeit with contingency plans understood and documented. Patrick

Lencioni supplies a helpful clarity-creation guide you can download here: http://bit.ly/2UFUmZ8

- Gamify commitment. To create a Leader Board, you must define a time-bound, cross-functional team goal. Once this is clear, you must cluster like roles or like strengths together into a subcommittee tasked with delivering a portion of the overall objective. In the story, Dave leverages the Clifton Strengths® assessment to define the team's leaders in the domains of execution, influencing, relationship building, and strategic thinking, and then divides the relevant tasks accordingly. The goals are then broken down into weekly key results to be delivered by each committee and scored. Winners receive the prized parking spots, and those bringing up the rear receive the cactus. Visit http://bit.ly/2Uq8yAi for a step-by-step guide to creating your own team Leader Board.

- Move forward. Norming teams routinely exercise the Five Ds: discussing, debating, deciding, doing, and diagnosing. Once decisions have been reached and agreed upon, it's essential that you move immediately into action—the doing phase. Storming teams have significant difficulty moving forward at pace because they revisit decisions constantly due to imperfect information. The way to enforce commitment once there is alignment on the goal is to measure the cadence of your team's action. There is a natural rhythm to execution in that every action leads the team one step closer (or further away from) achieving a result. Your role is to maintain forward momentum by visualizing team commitments to both the agreed norms and goals. On the goals side, a simple way to track continued commitment is to add a weekly completion percentage to the Leader Board, where each team member indicates their progress toward their goal in a status bar that might look like the following example:

Execution	Influence	Relationship Building	Strategic Thinking
Ensure achievement of all weekly milestones – Team Member 6	Benchmark against competiton – Team Member 2	Plan the team offsite – Team Member 3	Brainstorm 3 user-interface concepts –Team Member 7
Develop PR plan for prototype launch – Team Member 6	Edit and approve PR plan for prototype launch – Team Member 4	Ensure team social contract being followed by all members – Team Member 8	Complete market research with advisory group – Team Member 7
Complete the prototype – Team Member 1	Complete product communication pack – Team Member 2	Track and update team moodmeter each week – Team Member 8	Identify top 3 challenges that will prevent product prototype from launching successfully – Team Member 5

This type of progress visualization helps you understand the collective pace at which your team works and diagnose interdependencies that require greater shared commitment. In the example above, team members 1, 2, 7, and 8 are having issues keeping up with the pace set by team members 3, 5, and 6. If this isn't discussed, understood, and addressed, it could derail the team from achieving their goal.

Discussing this TPAP:

1. To what degree can your team align and move forward even if 100 percent consensus is not achieved?

2. What are your team's biggest dysfunctions when it comes to commitment?

3. How do you visualize the commitments that have been made and by whom?

4. What are the potential advantages of gamifying commitment for your teams?

5. How can you reward those who consistently keep their commitments and motivate those who do not?

TPAP #14 – Exercise Shared Accountability

In Chapter Ten, the team has arrived at the Goltur launch meeting in advance of Sam's arrival and is working feverishly to ensure every detail is ready for his inspection. For them to pull off a successful launch, each team member must know and own their role as individuals and as a team. Naturally there are obstacles to overcome, but by applying the collective talent of the team and exercising their shared norms, they successfully deliver the launch meeting. Ultimately, they receive high praise from the senior leaders of Giant, and their hard work is rewarded.

The true test of a norming team is the degree to which the leader must coach versus empower. Sam is enjoying the fruits of having a fully capable team, which allows him to focus on his own role during the launch meeting and not worry about which member(s) of his team will not fulfill their responsibilities. This type of empowerment sounds easy, but in reality it is quite difficult to accomplish because it is built on the back of trust, healthy debate, and full commitment. Even if all the pieces are solidly in place, things could still fall apart in the absence of shared accountability.

To prevent this, observe your team's behaviors when they encounter challenge. Teams have an ingrained accountability mechanism described in ***The Oz Principle*** by Craig Hickman, Roger Connors, and Tom Smith as "above the line or below the line."

Hickman, Connors, and Smith describe "below the line" attitudes as "the blame game," where the following behaviors manifest:

- Feigning ignorance
- Shifting focus
- Blaming and shaming others
- Requiring step-by-step directions
- Covering up mistakes
- Legitimizing delays

Conversely, "above the line" behaviors are as follows:

- Accepting the reality of the situation by obtaining the perspectives of others, being open and candid in communications, asking for and offering feedback, and hearing the hard things
- Taking ownership by being personally invested, learning from both successes and failures, aligning work with desired company results, and acting on feedback received
- Solving problems by regularly asking, "What else can I do?"; overcoming cross-functional boundaries; creatively dealing with obstacles; and taking the necessary risks
- Delivering by doing the things you say you'll do, focusing on the top priorities, not blaming others, and sustaining an environment of trust

Applying this TPAP:

- Play the victim. *The Oz Principle* provides an assessment
  to help each individual on your team determine if they
  have ever succumbed to "below the line" attitudes or
  behaviors. It's scored by giving yourself one point for
  every *Yes* response and zero points for every *No* response.
  The higher the score, the more self-aware you are about
  your potential failings. Once each team member takes
  the assessment, use the worksheet available at http://
  bit.ly/2vaznOP to populate the team's overall average
  so you can discuss how to take the group forward. The
  key to this exercise is that no matter how people score
  themselves or how the overall team fares, the realization
  needs to land that everyone succumbs to the victim cycle
  every now and again. The next part of the exercise is to
  have everyone complete the accountability scorecard
  here: http://bit.ly/2ILrVl8. They will rate each question
  from one (rarely exhibit) to three (usually exhibit). Once
  you have compiled the team assessment in tab two, you
  can identify the specific elements that need the greatest
  group improvement and develop actions to address them.

- Build a feedback culture. Openness and transparency
  are the antidotes to curing "below the line" behaviors.
  Feedback is a powerful tool to incentivize "above the
  line" behaviors and correct "below the line" actions. To
  leverage feedback effectively, use role play to increase
  comfort with the concept. Here is a simple one-hour

feedback workshop you can apply with your team: http://bit.ly/2Va6NvC

- Cement roles. A key part of solidifying team norms is to spell out roles for each team member. The RACI model is a straightforward tool used for identifying roles and responsibilities during a project. The acronym RACI stands for Responsible, Accountable, Consulted, and Informed. For every project or task there is usually a person or persons who do the work (responsible); those who supervise and ensure the correct and quality delivery of the work (accountable); those who assist by providing additional insights and information, like functional experts (consulted); and last but not least, those who need to be kept in the loop with regards to progress toward completion (informed). Without clearly defined roles and responsibilities, it is easy for projects to run into trouble. When people know what management expects of them, it is easier for them to complete their work on time, within budget, and to the right level of quality. A RACI matrix supports the model and is used to discuss, agree, and communicate roles and responsibilities.

In creating a RACI Matrix step-by-step (a template can be downloaded here: http://bit.ly/2PibAG2):

1. Identify all the tasks involved in delivering the project and list them on the left-hand side of the

chart in completion order.

2. Identify all the project roles and list them along the top of the chart.

3. Complete the cells of the chart, identifying who has the responsibility and the accountability, and who will be consulted and informed for each task.

4. Ensure every task has a responsible roleand an accountable role assigned to it.

5. No task should have more than one accountable role. Resolve any conflicts where there is more than one accountable person for a task.

6. Share, discuss, and agree on the RACI matrix with your stakeholders before your project starts.

• Visualize accountability. Once decisions are made, it is crucial to hold people accountable for delivering on their commitments. An accountability board is a simple tool that allows people to claim ownership of a given task. Plot the deliverables for a week, month, or quarter's activities and then ask your team members to commit to a deadline by placing a sticky note on a date. Doing this accomplishes two tasks: 1) it shows who may be overcommitted on your team, and 2) it shows who may be able to support more due to lack of involvement in key priorities. Review the accountability board each week and mark the sticky notes with either a green (completed) or red (incomplete) dot. As a team, discuss the red-dot items to understand why the deliverable was not achieved on time and what needs to happen to accelerate delivery.

Discussing this TPAP:

1. Would you rate your team's accountability behaviors as more "above the line" or "below the line"?

2. How capable are you and your team at giving and receiving positive and corrective feedback?

3. How disciplined is your team with regards to project and task management?

4. With what frequency does your team conduct progress reviews?

5. How much positive pressure is there within your team for poor performers to improve?

TPAP #15 – Execute until Achievement

By the epilogue, Sam and his team have successfully launched Goltur to the sales force, their internal stakeholders. Now the hard work really begins. The first-week numbers come in, and the trend is not where it should be. As mentioned in the last TPAP, team character is forged through the fires of disappointment and challenge. In Sam's case, he has built a team primed to conquer whatever trials they may encounter, but ultimately, they will be judged by their ability to execute with excellence.

As a leader, you should have garnered the general respect of your team by this point in your journey; they should truly believe that your intent is to serve and support them. You have unlocked the collective talent and potential of your group and aimed it at the collective goals you want to achieve by leveraging your shared openness, engaging in productive conflict, committing to decisions, and holding each other accountable. Still, the respect your team has for you will be proven by how well they adhere to established norms without you in the room. It is still quite common to see norming teams devolve into bad habits once the hard work starts.

Your job at this stage is to assess the degree to which your team remains focused on the team goal despite obstacles and competing priorities. The enemies of achievement are apathy and ego, and you must relentlessly weed out both if you are serious about accomplishing your objectives. Apathy represents the sense of achievement that comes from working amongst people you enjoy being with every day, which can become a surrogate for success. Ego comes into play with specific individuals who may feel they are more important to the success of the team than others, and who thus put their own achievements over those of the team.

Patrick Lencioni once again provides helpful guidance in ***The Five Dysfunctions of a Team***, stating that teams that fail to focus on results:

- Plateau
- Lose to the competition
- Cannot retain high achievers
- Reward individual achievements and promotions more than team achievements
- Lack laser focus on what really matters.

Conversely, teams that focus on shared outcomes:

- Develop and promote high achievers
- Reinforce team norms over individual desires
- Raucously celebrate wins and deeply grieve losses
- Make sacrifices for the good of the team
- Have crystal clarity and laser focus on what really matters.

All your collective work to arrive at this point will go down the drain if you don't make it explicit that collective results form the basis of how everyone's performance will be assessed. This should be made clear in the onboarding of each new team member and upheld as the king of the team's norms. Nothing matters if you fail to achieve your objective. In addition to apathy and ego, failure due to lack of shared focus and effort is extremely destructive to a fragile team's ecosystem.

Applying this TPAP:
- Never get too comfortable. If your collective goal is audacious enough, it will generate a pervasive "must do more" spirit in your team. In **Great by Choice**, Jim Collins refers to this as Level Five Ambition—passion for a cause larger than a team or organization, which infuses team members with the will to do whatever it takes to achieve their objective. But how do you know if your goal is level five? Well, go back to the *why* you defined back in TPAP #9. To meet the minimum standard, your goal should represent the intersection of deep passion, competitive advantage, and economic viability. The key here is to channel the team's ego and intensity into something bigger than any of you could ever achieve on your own. Check in regularly with your team to assess the degree to which the collective goal continues to motivate and energize everyone. At least once a year, survey your group on this topic and leverage the findings to refine your ambition or troubleshoot why you're not achieving the desired goal.

- Visualize progress. A team goal is merely the accumulation of a series of key achievements. Maintaining focus therefore requires you to align the necessary achievements that should add up to the desired results. In her book, **Radical Focus: Achieving Your Most Important Goals with Objectives and Key Results**, Christina Wodtke lays out an approach to inspire diverse teams to work together and go all out in pursuit of a single, challenging goal. Her system, called OKR (Objectives and Key Results), helps teams commit to bold goals and stay motivated despite setbacks and disappointments. In her parlance, an objective is defined as follows:
  - A single sentence that is both qualitative and inspirational, time-bound, and actionable by the team independently
  - Similar to a statement of purpose, but executable in less time. A well-elaborated objective motivates the team, is quite challenging (but doable) in a given amount of time, and can be executed by those who have agreed on it (e.g. *Make Goltur the most successful product launch in the category*)

Key Results are defined as tangible achievements that quantify the team's inspirational objective language. Key Results can be based on anything you can measure. You create them by asking a couple of simple questions:

  - How would we know if we met our objective? (e.g. *Goltur achieves 15 precent market share by the end of Q4*)

- ○ What numbers would change? (e.g. *New patient starts exceed last two category launches*)

The best measures are lead indicators, not lag indicators. A lead measure is one that is both predictive of future success and influenceable. Lag measures are the desired results. By aligning and acting on lead measures, you increase your team's focus on the achievements that will best help drive the objective. (e.g. *Lag measure: lose 20 pounds; Lead measures: decrease daily calorie intake and increase daily calories burned*)

To get started visualizing OKRs, download this Excel template: http://bit.ly/2UroMJE. If you want to collaborate online with your team, Weekdone.com offers a software service to help you along.

- Keep score. Ultimately, your team will be judged on its ability to execute until the desired results are achieved. The key to effective execution is to keep the team focused on a select few (no more than four or five) Wildly Important Goals (WIGs) with clearly articulated measures. Once the WIGs and measures are aligned, use a scoreboard to track achievement. Although scoreboards originally manifested as part of lean sigma practices in product-production businesses, they have become effective visual performance-management tools utilized by great teams in industries of all stripes. From Visual Workplace Inc., "Scoreboards summarize data that reveal opportunities for improvement and guide our problem-solving strategies. Scoreboards visually link data throughout the organization and establish a communication rhythm." The following are key questions to consider when building a scoreboard:

- Why is this information important to the organization? (The objective of the scoreboard should be defined and displayed with the scoreboard.)
- Who wants or needs to know this information?
- What information should be collected?
- Where will the data be displayed? (Scoreboards should be available at the point of use so that those collecting the data can help to recognize opportunities for improvement.)
- When will the information be reviewed?
- How will the information be gathered and displayed at the point of use?

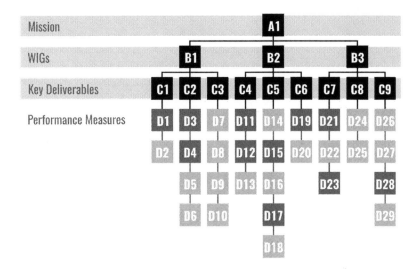

In the above example, you can see that the team is losing in several performance measures (shaded darker). The key to effectively applying a scoreboard once you have answered the questions above as a team is to leverage the score to drive your team into a problem-solving cycle.

What is our plan of action and timing plan?
Consider the timing, people, culture, environment

How effective is the solution?
Collate and analyse data – compare the results against the targets identified

Which option will resolve our problem and satisfy our constraints?
Set targets based on the anticipated impact the solution will have on the causes identified

Did our solution achieve our Desired State?
Whether it did or it didn't, it essential we understand why?

What options do we have?
Brainstorm & evaluate based on constraints identified

What do we want to improve, and where do we want to be?
Define the problem clearly.
Kipling and Open Questions
SMART

What is stopping us from achieving our Desired State?
Brainstorm & gather data
IDENTIFY THE ROOT CAUSE
Using Fishbone, Weighted Voting, Pareto, Check Sheet & 5 Why's

Implement Results Solution Desired State Structured Problem Solving Options Cause Problem

Executing until achievement requires that you and your team know where you are winning and losing, as well as why, so that you can quickly and sustainably improve when you are not achieving your goals. To accomplish this, you need to clearly articulate the problem, identify the root cause, generate options, decide on and implement agreed-upon solutions, and then quantify the impact of the actions.

Discussing this TPAP:

1. To what degree is your team focused on the achievement of shared objectives versus individual accolades?

2. How energized is your team by the shared objectives you need to achieve?

3. What is the current cadence of your team in terms of results orientation—fast-paced, plodding, or somewhere in between?

4. What are the most important success measures for your team?

5. How regularly does your team zoom in to specific areas of underperformance to diagnose and resolve root causes of challenges?

SECTION IV:

PERFORMING

Performing*

| 16. Foster Great Teamwork |
| 17. Inspect Expectations |
| 18. Reward And Recognize |
| 19. Continuous Improvement Mindset |
| 20. Stretch The Goalposts |

*covered in
Halo: The Mission of
High-Performance Teams

Preview: Performing

A norming team can occasionally win a championship but will endure difficulty to repeat the feat on a consistent basis. High performance happens when solid norms evolve into effective synergy. Performing teams are therefore more strategically aware and know clearly what they are doing, and why. They possess a shared vision and values and can stand on their own feet with no interference or participation from the leader. They focus on overachieving versus their goals. They have insights into personal and group processes and a better understanding of one another's strengths and weaknesses. Performing teams can resolve disagreements positively and make necessary changes to process and structure. Performing team members look out for each other. The leader's job once this stage is achieved is to delegate and oversee.

Leader Board: The DNA of High-Performance Teams is about creating the conditions for performance by systematically and methodically moving a group through the first three stages of the team formation process—forming, storming, and norming. If you've made it this far, then you have accumulated tons of useful tools, templates, and resources to skillfully guide your team to a point where higher performance is possible. Maintaining a sustainable performance culture is such an important topic, I decided to dedicate an entire book to the subject. ***Halo: The Mission of High-Performance Teams*** is a continuation of the Goltur marketing team's story, told through the eyes of Dave Maxwell.

Halo focuses on the practical application of five team performance-acceleration principles: fostering great teamwork, inspecting expectations, rewarding and recognizing performance, embedding the continuous-improvement mindset, and stretching the goalposts. This title will be published in 2020, and I hope you are as excited as I am to return to the world of Sam and his team when the book comes out.

RESOURCES

You can receive free access to all the resources available by visiting omarlharris.com and signing up on the File Share tab. If you are reading the print version of this book, you can access the same by using the following QR code:

If you do not wish to join the community of leaders on omarlharris.com and take advantage of constantly updated resources and useful content then you can access the Leader Board resources cloud at this url: http://bit.ly/LBresources.

ACKNOWLEDGMENTS

Leader Board would not exist if not for Mike McCann, one of the best leaders I've known in my career. Mike managed me from 2003-2006 and sparked and fed my hunger for knowledge about team management and leadership. He kept business books in his office, and I would borrow them on a regular basis. I discovered titles like *Good to Great* by Jim Collins through Mike. During a discussion in his office in 2006, very early on in my professional career, we first conversed about cementing some of the things that made our team so special—including the team Leader Board we'd innovated.

We brainstormed a whole series of business books, written in narrative style, about a fictional business team trying to overcome the odds to achieve greatness. Mike knew I was a writer—at the time, I was trying to complete my first fiction novel, *One Blood* (under the pseudonym Qwantu Amaru). He encouraged me to consider drafting the first of our business books too, so I jotted down the basic concept and even wrote a few chapters, but nothing more, back in 2006.

Ten years later, I was living in Jakarta, Indonesia, working as a general manager at a large pharmaceutical company, and I realized that it was time to start the series. In the intervening years, I had transformed from individual contributor to enterprise leader and was now facing the toughest test of my career—my first time leading an organization of nearly nine hundred people in a foreign country and culture. As I matriculated through my first ninety days on the job, I kept going back to experiences gained while working on that great team from 2003 to 2009. I was still applying learnings from a team-building session in 2005—principally the four stages of team formation, Clifton Strengths®, and Patrick Lencioni's ***The Five Dysfunctions of a Team***.

I've never been great at keeping a journal, but ***Leader Board*** became my journal of sorts. I wanted to do two things with the book: 1) memorialize and express my deep gratitude for that great team on which I had the opportunity to work, and 2) crystallize twelve years of my own hard-won knowledge from applying the advice of leadership thought leaders while leading teams in the US, Brazil, the Middle East, and Indonesia in large corporations and small start-ups. When it comes to the first objective, there are so many people I must thank for the kinship, camaraderie, and fun times we had while working very hard to achieve our collective objectives.

First, I need to thank Ray Russo, my own real-life version of Coach, a man whose infectious zeal for life pervaded every moment of our working relationship. With Ray, you never felt you were working *under* him but rather *alongside* him. I hope you enjoyed the *very* fictionalized version of our story, Ray! Ray's boss at the time was Sean McNicholas—an "*O captain, my captain*" sort of leader who inspired fierce loyalty and high performance, someone who personally saw to it that I was continuously stretched in the early stages of my career. Thank you, Sean, wherever you are! Tracey Gibson was the reason I made it on the team in the first place. Without her strong endorsement to Ray, I never would have stood a chance, so she literally changed my life. Thanks, Tracey! We had a great cross-functional team, and I have dedicated this book to that entire group—it really did take a village!

Leader Board would also not exist without the brilliant thinking of the many leadership gurus I have learned from over the years. While not an exhaustive list, I owe each of these thought leaders a debt of gratitude: First, I must thank Donald O. Clifton, the father of positive psychology, author of *How Full is Your Bucket*, and founder of the global strengths movement. I was introduced to the latter at the beginning of my professional career (thanks to Tom Manos), and it has been the fuel in my jetpack ever since. I cannot overstate the importance of Clifton Strengths® to my own personal career journey, and I owe it all to Mr. Clifton's groundbreaking work. I also want to thank Mr. Clifton's organization, Gallup, for advancing the strengths-based management cause and author Tom Rath for the excellent lessons in *StrengthsFinder 2.0* and *Strengths Based Leadership*.

Next, I need to thank Stephen R. Covey for the exceptionally influential *7 Habits of Highly Effective People*. Continuing this gratitude train, I want to also thank Jim Collins and the *Good to Great* and *Great by Choice* research teams. I have internalized their lessons to the point of personal dogma! I need to recognize James C. Hunter for writing his impactful book about love and leadership, *The Servant*. John C. Maxwell has forgotten more about leadership than I will ever know, but I specifically must appreciate him for *The 21 Irrefutable Laws of Leadership*, *The 17 Indisputable Laws of Teamwork*, and *Everyone Communicates, Few Connect*.

If you've read *The 5 Dysfunctions of a Team*, then you know just how much influence Patrick Lencioni has had in forming my own team leadership foundations. Were it not for his leadership fable, I would not have had the courage to create my own. His books should be required reading for anyone who even thinks they want to lead. His organization, The Table Group, has produced a wealth of resources that I recommend everyone reading this investigate more fully.

Other luminaries I need to recognize are Dale Carnegie, author of *How to Make Friends and Influence People* and creator of the course *How to Communicate with Diplomacy and Tact*; Bruce Tuckman, author of the 1965 article "Developmental Sequence in Small Groups"; Simon Sinek, author of *Start with Why*; Ron Friedman, author of *The Best Place to Work*; Michael Margolis, author of *Believe Me*; Christina Wodtke, author of *Radical Focus;* Dennis and Michelle Reina, authors of *Trust and Betrayal in the Workplace*; and Craig Hickman, Roger Connors, and Tom Smith, authors of *The Oz Principle*. By amalgamating and connecting the important work of each of them, I've accelerated my success with teams in my day job while reinforcing the team performance acceleration principles within this book.

Without my amazing team at TPC Books, Stephanie Casher and James W. Lewis, none of my writing would see the light of day. We've been riding this independent publishing train together since 2009, and I don't think we're stopping anytime soon. My test readers were instrumental in shaping and guiding the final form of this book: Andrew Miles, Mike McCann, Thomas Halusa, Iveta Goda Degulyte, JD Capuano, Dahlia Sutrisno, Sylvia Aziz, Vishrut Awasthi, Jayson Lo, Federico Barreto, and Burcu Kaylan Miles—thank you so much for supporting me! Reedsy.com was fundamental in terms of sourcing an amazing internal illustrator, Michael Rehder; copy-editor extraordinaire Lynsey Griswold, and interior book designer, Vanessa Mendozzi. Cathi Stevenson of BookCoverExpress.com developed the amazing cover! And permissions work was conducted by Cheryl Cooper.

Of course, I need to thank my wonderful family, who have watched me wander around the world hoping it would make sense (and cents) at some point. My parents, Samuel and Sameerah Harris, were my first and still best teachers of leadership; my sister, Sameerah, teaches me about personal resilience every day; my brothers, Kamau, Patrick, and John, have set important examples for me my whole life; my aunt Janis, my niece Kiarra (and great nieces Egypt and Empress), and my nephew Hamilton—I do all this for you!

Lastly, to all you leaders out there, whether you are new to the job or have been doing it for decades—I hope you believe as I do that we as leaders can (and must) learn how to tap into and unlock our teams' DNA to achieve breakout results. We are facing a crisis of employee engagement globally, and the only way to overcome the tremendous challenges we will face within our companies and societies is to stand side by side, full of trust and commitment, and execute together until we get the job done. I look forward to continuing to build a legion of empowered leaders to confront whatever obstacles may come. I hope I can count on you to join me in the fight. Lastly, if you found value in this book, please pass it on to a friend and review it on Amazon.com!

Omar L. Harris
February 28, 2019
São Paulo, Brazil

ABOUT THE AUTHOR

Omar L. Harris hails from Pittsburgh, PA, and is passionate about leading teams, high-performance coaching, and
inspiring the future leaders of today and tomorrow. He is a
Gallup Certified Strengths Coach; a bestselling, award-win-
ning author; independent publishing guru; entrepreneur; and
twenty-year veteran of the global pharmaceutical industry with
stints at Pfizer, Schering-Plough, Merck, GSK, and Allergan,
while living in the US, Brazil, the Middle East, and South-
east Asia. He is the author of three titles: *One Blood* (under
pseudonym Qwantu Amaru), ***From Authors to Entrepreneurs***
(with co-authors Stephanie Casher and James W. Lewis), and

Leader Board: The DNA of High-Performance Teams. Omar is quite active on social media, and you can join his mailing list and/or follow him on his personal website, LinkedIn, Facebook, Twitter, and Instagram. He currently resides in São Paulo, Brazil, working as General Manager of Allergan PLC. In addition to this demanding day job, he is hard at work on the sequel to this book—*Halo: The Mission of High-Performance Teams.*

www.omarlharris.com

Linkedin: omarlharris/
Facebook: @authorleadercoach
Twitter: @strengthsleader
Instagram: omarl.harris_agn

APPENDIX

REFERENCES

Foreword: Team DNA

1. Bruce W. Tuckman. "Developmental Sequence in Small Groups." *Psychological Bulletin*, 1965, Vol. 63, No. 6, 386-387.

Chapter One: The Negativity Trap

2. Donald O. Clifton and Tom Rath. ***How Full is Your Bucket?*** Gallup Press, 2004. Chapter One: The Theory of the Dipper and the Bucket.

3. Clifton and Rath, Chapter Six: Strategy Two: Shine a Light on What's Right.

Chapter Two: Take Control

4. Stephen R. Covey. ***The 7 Habits of Highly Effective People: Powerful Lessons in Personal Change***. Mango Publishing Group, 1989. pg. 73.

5. Covey, 78.

6. Covey, 76-79.

7. Covey, 83.

8. Covey, 83, 93.

9. Covey, 83, 93.

10. Covey, 92.

Chapter Three: W.H.O.M.

11. Jim Collins. *Good to Great: Why Some Companies Make the Leap and Others Don't*. Harper Business, 2001. pg. 41-42

Chapter Four: Servant Leadership

12. James C. Hunter. *The Servant: A Simple Story About the True Essence of Leadership*. Random House, 2008. Back cover synopsis.

Chapter Five: Intense Intent

13. John C. Maxwell. *Everyone Communicates, Few Connect: What the Most Effective People Do Differently*. Thomas Nelson, 2010. pg. 89.
14. Maxwell, 2010. Connecting principles are the chapter headings in this book.
15. John C. Maxwell. *The 21 Irrefutable Laws of Leadership: Follow Them and People Will Follow You*. Thomas Nelson, 2007. pg. 1.
16. Maxwell, 5-7.
17. Maxwell, 7-9.

Chapter Six: Star Search

18. Tom Rath. *StrengthsFinder 2.0.* Gallup Press, 2013. Kindle ebook location 146-360.
19. Rath, location 271.
20. Rath, location 286.
21. Clifton StrengthsFinder THEMES. Copyright ©

2000, 2012 Gallup, Inc. All rights reserved. Gallup®, StrengthsFinder, Clifton StrengthsFinder, and each of the 34 Clifton StrengthsFinder theme names are trademarks of Gallup, Inc.

22. Tom Rath. *Strengths Based Leadership: Great Leaders, Teams, and Why People Follow*. Gallup Press, 2009. pg 22-26.

23. Gallup. "Guide for Strengths-Based Discussions in Organizations." Copyright © 2007 Gallup, Inc. All rights reserved.

Chapter Seven: Basic Brilliance

24. James F. Anderson, Laronistine Dyson, Jerald C. Burns. *Boot Camps: An Intermediate Sanction*. University Press of America, 1999.

25. Jim Collins. *Good to Great: Why Some Companies Make the Leap and Others Don't*. Harper Business, 2001. pg. 95.

26. Collins, 90-92.

Chapter Nine: Productive Conflict

27. Patrick Lencioni. *The Five Dysfunctions of a Team: A Leadership Fable*. Jossey-Bass; 2003. pg. 187.

Chapter Ten: Know and Own Your Role

28. John C. Maxwell. *The 17 Essential Qualities of a Team Player: Becoming the Kind of Person Every Team Wants*. Thomas Nelson, 2006. Image adapted

from chapter titles 1-17.

TPAP #1: Hire the Right W.H.O.M.

29. Glassdoor.com. *Free Ebook: How to Write Great Job Descriptions That Land You Great Hires*. 2014. Page 2.

30. Ron Friedman. *The Best Place to Work: The Art and Science of Creating an Extraordinary Workplace*. TarcherPerigee, 2014, pg. 114.

TPAP #2: Control over Concern

31. Jim Collins, Morten T. Hansen. *Great by Choice: Uncertainty, Chaos, and Luck—Why Some Thrive Despite Them All*. Harper Business, 2011. Ebook location 424-465.

TPAP #3: Serve and Support

32. James C. Hunter. *The Servant: A Simple Story About the True Essence of Leadership*. Random House, 2008. Back cover synopsis.

TPAP #4: Fill Buckets Daily

33. Donald O. Clifton and Tom Rath. *How Full is Your Bucket?* Gallup Press, 2004.

TPAP #6: Raise Your Leadership Lid

34. John C. Maxwell. *The 21 Irrefutable Laws of Leadership: Follow Them and People Will Follow*

You. Thomas Nelson, 2007. pg. 1-10.

35. Mike Myatt. "Think You're A Leader? Take the Test and Find Out." Forbes.com, 2012. http://www.forbes.com/sites/mikemyatt/2012/05/22/think-youre-a-leader-take-the-test-and-find-out.

TPAP #7: Derive Team DNA

36. Tom Rath. ***StrengthsFinder 2.0***. Gallup Press, 2013. Kindle ebook location 269.

TPAP #9: WHY Before WHAT

37. Simon Sinek. ***Start With Why: How Great Leaders Inspire Everyone to Take Action***. Penguin Group, 2009. pg. 41.

TPAP #10: Connect the Dots

38. Ron Friedman. ***The Best Place to Work: The Art and Science of Creating an Extraordinary Workplace***. TarcherPerigee, 2014, pg. 129.

39. John C. Maxwell. ***Everyone Communicates, Few Connect: What the Most Effective People Do***. Thomas Nelson, 2010. pg 96-11.

TPAP #11: Enhance Team Trust

40. Dennis Reina, Michelle Reina. ***Trust and Betrayal in the Workplace: Building Effective Relationships in Your Organization***. Berrett-Koehler Publishers Inc., 2015. pg. 22, 45, 77.

41. Patrick Lencioni. *The Five Dysfunctions of a Team: A Leadership Fable*. Jossey-Bass, 2003. pg 196-197.

TPAP #12: Encourage Productive Conflict

42. Dale Carnegie. *How to Communicate with Diplomacy and Tact*. AMA course. https://www.dalecarnegie.com/en/courses/diplomacy-and-tact.

43. Amy Galo. *HBR Guide to Dealing with Conflict*. Harvard Business Review Press. 2016.

44. Patrick Lencioni. *The Five Dysfunctions of a Team: A Leadership Fable*. Jossey-Bass, 2003. pg 207.

45. Lencioni, 209-210.

TPAP #14: Exercise Shared Accountability

46. Roger Connors, Tom Smith, Craig Hickman. *The Oz Principle: Getting Results Through Individual and Organizational Accountability*. Penguin Group, 1998. Ebook location 190-203.

47. Connors, Smith, and Hickman, location 553 to 2373.

TPAP #15: Execute until Achievement

48. Patrick Lencioni. *The Five Dysfunctions of a Team: A Leadership Fable*. Jossey-Bass, 2003. pg 21.

49. Christina Wodtke. *Radical Focus: Achieving Your Most Important Goals with Objectives and Key Results*. Amazon Digital Services, 2016.

50. Visual Workplace Inc. "VISUAL management techniques to create effective SCOREBOARDs

for your workplace environment." https://www.visualworkplaceinc.com/2015/04/visual-management-techniques-to-create-effective-scoreboards-for-your-workplace-environment/.

CHARACTERS

Giant Pharmaceuticals
Senior Leadership Team (SLT)

- Myra Khan – Chief Executive Officer
- Carl Reed – President
- Luke Stockley – Chief Operating Officer
- Richard de Fiore – Chief Financial Officer
- Carter Henson – Senior Vice President of Legal
- Samantha Parker – Senior Vice President of Communications
- Brian Woodstock – Chief Information Officer

Giant Pharmaceuticals US Goltur/Induet
Marketing Team

- James (Jim) Kelly – Global Vice President, Marketing
- Samuel "Coach" Lombardi – Senior Director, Marketing
- Dave Maxwell – Director, Marketing
- Robert Rath – Director, Marketing
- Alicia Barden – Associate Product Manager
- Lincoln Stephens – Associate Product Manager
- Marcus Gleeson – Associate Market Access Manager

- Rebecca Abrams – Communications Manager
- Gaile Deegan – Executive Assistant

Giant Pharmaceuticals Global Goltur/Induet Marketing Team

- Scott Denger – Senior Director, Global Marketing
- Greg Bundy – Director, Global Market Access
- Vignesh Neeru – Associate Product Manager

Giant Pharmaceuticals Cholesterol Cross-Functional Team

- Hank Lowenstein – Vice President, Direct-To-Consumer Advertising
- Karen Salinger – Public Relations Director
- Sarah Richardson – Analytics Director
- Larry Streeter – Managed Care Director
- Dan Sarver – Marketing Operations Director
- Alexandra Lubantik – Vice President, Finance
- Nate Spinola – Finance Director
- Chuck Towns – HR Director
- Luca Rizzo – Cardiovascular Research & Development Head

Made in the USA
Middletown, DE
13 May 2019